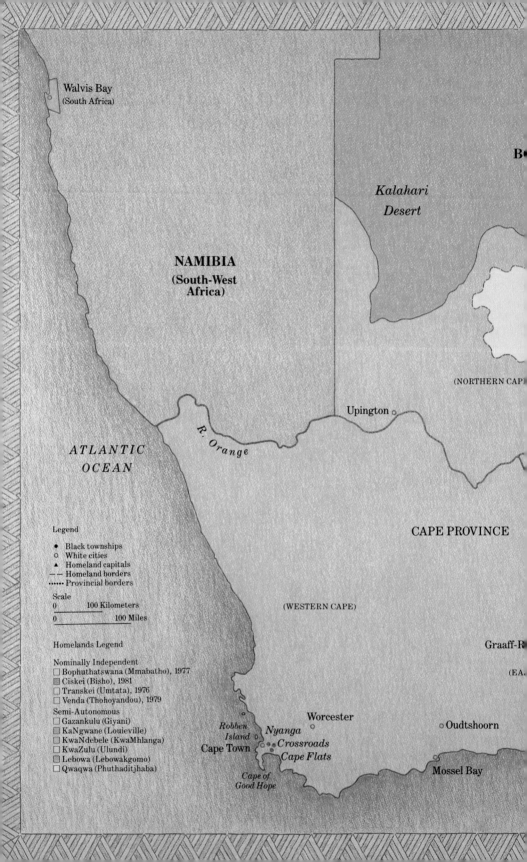

Walvis Bay
(South Africa)

B●

Kalahari
Desert

NAMIBIA
(South-West
Africa)

(NORTHERN CAP

Upington ○

*ATLANTIC
OCEAN*

R. Orange

CAPE PROVINCE

Legend
● Black townships
○ White cities
▲ Homeland capitals
– – Homeland borders
••••• Provincial borders

Scale
0 _____ 100 Kilometers
0 _____ 100 Miles

Homelands Legend

Nominally Independent
□ Bophuthatswana (Mmabatho), 1977
■ Ciskei (Bisho), 1981
□ Transkei (Umtata), 1976
□ Venda (Thohoyandou), 1979
Semi-Autonomous
□ Gazankulu (Giyani)
□ KaNgwane (Louieville)
□ KwaNdebele (KwaMhlanga)
□ KwaZulu (Ulundi)
□ Lebowa (Lebowakgomo)
□ Qwaqwa (Phuthaditjhaba)

(WESTERN CAPE)

Graaff-R

(EA.

Worcester ○   ○ Oudtshoorn

Robben   *Nyanga*
Island ○ ○●*Crossroads*
Cape Town *Cape Flats*

*Cape of
Good Hope*   Mossel Bay

Minerals Legend
Au Gold
Co Cobalt
Cr Chromium
Cu Copper
Fe Iron
Mn Manganese
Ni Nickel
Pl Platinum
Ti Titanium
U   Uranium
V   Vanadium
C   Coal
D   Diamonds
O   Oil

R. Congo (Zaire)

ZAIRE

Kisangani

Au

Cu

Au

Ilebo

Cabinda

O

Kinshasa

D

D

D

D

C

Co

U

Cu

*Lake
Victoria*

*Lake
Tanganyika*

Kigoma

TANZANIA

Dar es
Salaam

Luanda

Cu

Mn

O

Fe

Mn

Malanje

Luso

Huambo

Co

Lubumbashi

Mn

Co

MALAWI

Lilongwe

*Lake
Malawi*

Fe

Lobito

Benguela

Fe

ANGOLA

Zambezi R.

ZAMBIA

Lusaka

Co
Cu

U

Mn

Nacala

Blantyre

Namibe

Fe

Livingstone

Jamba

Cu

Cr

Au

C

C

Harare

1

2

Caprivi Strip

ZIMBABWE

Au

Cu

Au

Cr

Mutare

Beira

Grootfontein

Cu

V

V

**NAMIBIA
(South-West
Africa)**

Mn

Walvis Bay
(South Africa)

Windhoek

Lake Malawi

Bulawayo

D

Ni
Cu

Au

Au

C

Cr

MOZAMBIQUE

R. Limpopo

BOTSWANA

Gaborone

Mn

Ni

Pt

Au

Fe

Cr

Cu

Cr

D

Pretoria

Au

Fe

Maputo

Lüderitz

D

D

V

Johannesburg

Fe

Kimberley

Mn

Au

U

Bloemfontein

C

C

SWAZILAND

Richard's Bay

D

D

U

D

U

D

D

R. Orange

Cu

**SOUTH
AFRICA**

C

Durban

LESOTHO

*ATLANTIC
OCEAN*

Saldanha

Cape Town

East London

Port Elizabeth

*INDIAN
OCEAN*

Legend
••• Major Roads
•• Major Roads/Railroads
⊢⊦ Major Railroads
═ Pipelines
1 Cahora Bassa Dam
2 Kariba Dam

Scale
0   200 Kilometers

0 ⸻ 200 Miles

SOUTHERN
AFRICA

THE UNITED STATES AND SOUTH AFRICA: THE REAGAN YEARS

THE UNITED STATES AND SOUTH AFRICA: THE REAGAN YEARS

PAULINE H. BAKER

SOUTH AFRICA **UPDATE** SERIES
FORD FOUNDATION—FOREIGN POLICY ASSOCIATION

Copublished by the Ford Foundation and the Foreign Policy Association

© Copyright 1989 by the Ford Foundation

Printed in the United States of America
Library of Congress Catalogue Card Number: 89-81063
ISBN: 0-87124-129-3

Book design by Samuel N. Antupit
Map design and illustration by Lea Cyr

South Africa UPDATE Series

CONTENTS

PREFACE

In 1981 the Study Commission on U.S. Policy Toward Southern Africa, funded by the Rockefeller Foundation and chaired by Franklin A. Thomas, published the results of a two-year study entitled *South Africa: Time Running Out (SATRO)*. The report contained an extensive review of South Africa's history, people, economy, and social and political systems; a survey of South Africa's relations with its neighbors and the rest of the world; and interviews with South Africans across racial, religious, and economic lines. The study concluded with an analysis of U.S. interests in South Africa and laid out a framework for U.S. policy in southern Africa, with specific objectives and actions for U.S. public and private groups. *SATRO* has been reprinted and has become a seminal teaching and reference resource. It is probably still the most comprehensive treatment of South Africa and U.S. policy available.

Since 1981 events in southern Africa have moved swiftly and the United States has become more involved in the region. The political crisis in South Africa has deepened, with no clear path to a solution in sight. The region has experienced considerable conflict and human suffering as well as hopeful signs of peace. The international climate has changed, with the superpowers moving toward cooperation on regional and other issues. In the United States, southern Africa has aroused growing interest and become a prominent fixture on the foreign policy agenda.

Many parts of *SATRO* consequently have become dated, although others, particularly the policy section, remain relevant. It was therefore decided to update the work with a series of publications covering the period from 1980 to the present. The new books use *South Africa: Time Running Out* as a point of departure yet are sufficiently comprehensive to be read independently. The concept behind the series is to produce a thorough journal of record and an analytical resource for teachers, students, and policymakers as well as a broader audience. Each book deals with a single topic related to South Africa and is written by one or more specialists. In addition to the text, each book contains a summary of the relevant chapter of *SATRO*, a topical chronology and bibliography, a chronology of key events in South African history, an annotated general bibliography on South Africa, appendices, and maps.

The South Africa UPDATE series is co-published by the Ford Foundation and the Foreign Policy Association. It is produced under the aegis of the Ford Foundation's Southern Africa Study Group and the guidance of an editorial board consisting of academics; former U.S. government and UN officials; business, labor, and foundation executives; and journalists. The opinions expressed in the books, however, are those of the authors.

John de St. Jorre
Editor
South Africa UPDATE Series

SUMMARY, *South Africa: Time Running Out,*
Chapter 16, "The United States and South Africa"

Truman Administration (1945–53). South Africa emerged as a foreign policy issue for the United States at the United Nations in the early 1950s, when other nations criticized the United States for its racial practices and for its failure to condemn apartheid.

Eisenhower Administration (1953–61). In the mid-1950s civil rights activism at home and the emergence of independent black states in Africa stimulated a more critical U.S. posture toward South Africa. The Sharpeville shootings on March 21, 1960, caused a hardening of U.S. rhetoric and a temporary withdrawal of American capital, but military, nuclear, intelligence, trade, and investment links between the two countries continued uninterrupted.

Kennedy Administration (1961–63). Africa was given a new prominence in foreign policy. G. Mennen Williams, a leading member of the Democratic party's liberal wing, was put in charge of African affairs at the State Department. Anti-apartheid criticism increased and relations with Pretoria cooled. The United States imposed a unilateral arms embargo against South Africa, effective January 1, 1964, but trade, investment, and intelligence cooperation remained intact.

Johnson Administration (1963–69). Kennedy's South Africa policy was strengthened by tightening the arms embargo, prohibiting sales of material that had dual civilian and military use, continuing the policy of "neither encouraging nor discouraging" U.S. investment, and banning U.S. naval ships from visiting South African ports. The United States pressed the UN Security Council for "effective measures" to obtain Namibia's independence, but balked at taking stronger action against South Africa, such as sanctions.

Nixon Administration (1969–74). U.S.–South African relations were placed in the context of wider strategic considerations. This was embodied in

National Security Study Memorandum 39 (NSSM 39), one of a number of U.S. foreign policy reviews ordered by Henry Kissinger, the president's national security adviser. Of the five policy options offered by NSSM 39, Kissinger chose the one that subordinated African rights and moral issues to U.S. economic and geopolitical interests. Just as a concern for civil rights and support from black leaders had contributed to Kennedy's and Johnson's measured opposition to South Africa, Nixon's "southern strategy" of courting racial conservatives made closer ties with Pretoria more attractive.

Evidence of a policy shift included resumption of gray-area sales of light planes, helicopters, and communications equipment; relaxation of restrictions on Export-Import Bank financing; exchanges of high-level officials; a softening of U.S. criticism of Pretoria at the United Nations; and the White House's refusal to back the State Department in lobbying against the Byrd Amendment, which removed the U.S. ban on Rhodesian chrome.

From South Africa's viewpoint, the most important American initiative was to free gold from its fixed price of $35 an ounce and let it float upward. Although the decision was made for reasons that had nothing to do with South Africa, it had the effect of strengthening Pretoria's capacity to withstand international economic pressures.

Ford Administration (1974–77). The 1974 military coup in Portugal, which led to the independence of Angola and Mozambique under Marxist governments, marked a turning point in U.S.–southern African affairs. Kissinger adopted a more active and flexible approach to southern Africa, focusing on Rhodesia. He enlisted the help of the African "frontline" states as well as South Africa. Ian Smith agreed to the principle of majority rule within two years and to negotiations with black nationalist movements, but subsequent talks in Geneva collapsed in late 1976.

Carter Administration (1977–81). A broad reassessment was made of international and domestic trends affecting foreign policy with the intention of changing both the style and substance of the administration's African policy. Carter and many of his closest advisers saw African nationalism, not Communist aggression, as the driving historical force in southern Africa, a force deemed largely consonant with American interests.

The differences between the new administration and Pretoria became obvious at a meeting between Vice President Walter Mondale and Prime Minister John Vorster in Vienna in early 1977, when Mondale made it clear that the United States supported majority rule in South Africa. Later in the year, relations deteriorated sharply between the two countries. The main reasons were the detection of a suspected nuclear weapons test site in the Kalahari by the Soviet Union and Pretoria's crackdown on opposition movements following the death in detention of Steve Biko, the "Black Consciousness" leader. The United States joined other major countries at the United Nations in imposing a mandatory arms embargo against South Africa in November 1977.

Diplomatic contacts continued as the Carter administration worked for the independence of Rhodesia and Namibia. A joint British–U.S. initiative to negotiate Rhodesia's independence was launched but failed to produce a solution. However, Zimbabwe became independent in 1980 through a subsequent British initiative backed by the United States. The five Western members of the UN Security Council (the United States, Britain, France, West Germany, and Canada) formed themselves into the "Contact Group," which worked closely with the United Nations, South Africa, the South-West African People's Organization (SWAPO), and other interested parties to achieve a settlement in Namibia. A plan for a cease-fire and UN-supervised elections was drawn up and approved by the UN Security Council as Resolution 435, but implementation was rejected by South Africa at a conference in Geneva in January 1981.

Changes in the style of U.S. policy were clear under Carter, but substantive shifts were less obvious, particularly in the second half of the term, when the administration became wary of Soviet and Cuban intentions in southern Africa. Internally divided, the Carter administration often sent confusing signals to South Africa and to its domestic audience. While its anti-apartheid rhetoric was strong, the Carter administration seemed reluctant to end all nuclear cooperation with South Africa, unclear about what it expected white South Africans to do and at what pace, unwilling to consider the threat of economic sanctions, and inclined to encourage U.S. businesses to stay and play an active role in South Africa.

THE UNITED STATES AND SOUTH AFRICA: THE REAGAN YEARS

Introduction

Until the 1980s, U.S. policy toward southern Africa had traveled a relatively well-defined path, with objectives that, in general, aroused little public debate. Successive administrations opposed apartheid and urged peaceful political change in South Africa. They sought to bring about the independence of the white-ruled states of Rhodesia and Namibia, to diminish Soviet influence in southern Africa, and to stabilize the region. Each administration rejected broad economic sanctions as a means of pressuring the South African government and urged South Africa, albeit unsuccessfully, to open its nuclear facilities to international inspection by signing the Nuclear Non-Proliferation Treaty. No administration contemplated lifting the U.S. arms embargo on South Africa or recognizing the "independent homelands" set aside for Africans by Pretoria.

The Reagan administration's goals in South Africa and the region were similar to its predecessors'. However, its strategy was different and highly controversial. Calling its policy "constructive engagement," the administration chose to work quietly with the South African government, stressing common strategic interests, empathizing with white fears, and utilizing a unilateral rather than a multilateral approach to diplomatic negotiations. The administration justified this new approach with the argument that the Carter administration, which had been more confrontational in its dealings with Pretoria, had lost momentum in pursuing its policy objectives—a charge strongly denied by Carter officials. It also believed that its conservative credentials placed it in a unique position to influence the South African government.

During its first term, the Reagan administration concentrated on regional diplomacy, with Namibia's independence given top priority. However, this longstanding problem was approached from a new angle—by formally tying South Africa's withdrawal from the territory, under a UN plan negotiated during the Carter administration, to the removal of Cuban forces from Angola. The purpose of "linkage," as it came to be known, was to address South Africa's security concerns while providing it with an incentive to surrender territory it regarded as a buffer against insurgency and international communism. A Cuban withdrawal was also consistent with the administration's strong desire to reduce Communist influence in the Third World.

However, South Africa, while participating in diplomatic negotiations, launched a campaign of military and economic aggression against neighboring states, undermining the administration's efforts to bring stability to the region. Nonetheless, by the end of Reagan's first term in 1984, the United States had brokered the Lusaka Agreement (a limited security pact between South Africa and Angola) and the Nkomati Accord (a broader nonaggression treaty between South Africa and Mozambique). As a result, the administration claimed some progress in resolving the region's conflicts, even though those agreements soon broke down.

In Reagan's second term, the administration's focus shifted from diplomacy in southern Africa to coping with domestic political challenges to its policies from both the left and the right. Before Reagan, administrations had dealt with South Africa in the context of a relatively calm domestic environment. Although there had long been active and often highly vocal lobbies on both sides of the issue, South Africa had a relatively low priority on the foreign policy agenda and had never occupied the center of the political stage.

In the mid-1980s, however, South Africa emerged as one of the most prominent and divisive foreign policy debates of the Reagan period. Four interrelated factors were primarily responsible. First, the highly publicized black South African uprising against apartheid, which began in September 1984 and lasted for more than two years before subsiding into sporadic protests, sensitized Americans to the human rights issues in the South African conflict and the depth of black frustration. Second, grassroots initiatives in the United States, in which the growing political power of American blacks was a major force, transformed public sentiment into sustained political action that pushed Congress into a direct confrontation with the administration. Third, President Reagan's own idiosyncratic views of South Africa, combined with conflicts over policy inside the administration and within the Republican Party, confused the debate, undermined the president's supporters in Congress, and gave ammunition to the anti-apartheid movement.

Finally, the failure of constructive engagement to produce tangible results left the policy virtually defenseless when it came under concerted attack. In spite of the United States' sympathetic approach, the South African government refused to address the central issue of black political rights; Namibia remained under South African control; the number of Cubans in Angola increased substantially; and violence escalated throughout the region. Indeed, South Africa seemed to have become an adversary of the United States rather than the regional ally originally envisioned by the Reagan administration.

The result was the passage of the Comprehensive Anti-Apartheid Act (CAAA) in October 1986, which demonstrated that South Africa had become a major political issue for the first time. This landmark legislation, passed over the veto of a popular president, mandated selective economic sanctions against South Africa. Although the Reagan administration continued to oppose sanctions, it did make some tactical adjustments in its policies toward South Africa and the region after the legislation was enacted. These were designed primarily to meet domestic and African criticism that the United States was on the side of the whites in South Africa and to strengthen its bona fides as a mediator in the Namibian and Angolan conflicts. While public interest in South Africa waned, conservative and liberal groups remained active, the former urging greater support for antigovernment guerrillas in Angola and Mozambique, and the latter pressing for further sanctions against South Africa.

During the last year of the Reagan presidency, the policy focus returned to Namibia and Angola, bringing the administration back to where it had started in 1981. Changing military and economic realities in southern Africa and a more collaborative relationship between the United States and the Soviet Union created an opportunity for the United States to revive its diplomatic initiative. A series of complex negotiations by Angola, Cuba, and South Africa, brokered by the United States, took place during 1988. The outcome was the signing of two interlocking treaties at the United Nations in December. South Africa agreed to withdraw from Namibia and to permit the UN to supervise preindependence elections; Angola agreed to send all the Cuban troops home.

The treaties, however, did not end the civil war in Angola, and the amount of time designated for their implementation—a total of twenty-seven months—raised fears of possible mishaps or a change of heart by the signatories. Nevertheless, the accords were an important benchmark in regional diplomacy and raised hopes for peace throughout the region. Implementation would take the vexing issue of Namibia, Africa's last colony, off the international agenda and end Cuban involvement in Angola, removing a major irritant to U.S.-Soviet relations. The change in Soviet attitudes also seemed to offer new opportunities for policymakers.

Internally, South Africa seemed to have reached a political stalemate in which black opposition had not been victorious, crushed, or co-opted and the government had retained its power but was drifting without direction.

Reagan's First Term: The Rise of Constructive Engagement

The Reagan administration sought to distinguish itself from its predecessor by drawing lines of contrast in both style and substance. Where Jimmy Carter made southern Africa one of his top foreign policy priorities and gave it a high public profile during his presidency, Ronald Reagan tucked the region into the background and stressed "quiet diplomacy." Where Carter emphasized human rights and worked on multilateral diplomatic initiatives, Reagan played up the threat of communism and adopted a more unilateral approach. And where Carter became personally involved and appointed a team of advisers to shape his policy, Reagan remained largely aloof from the issue and depended primarily on one individual— Assistant Secretary of State for African Affairs Chester A. Crocker.

Chester Arthur Crocker, forty years old when he took office, seemed a logical choice for the top African job in the State Department in a Republican administration. He had worked under Henry Kissinger in the National Security Council and had been a foreign policy adviser to Vice President George Bush during his campaign for the 1980 Republican presidential nomination. During the Carter administration, he was director of African Studies at Georgetown University's Center for Strategic and International Studies, specializing in southern African military and political affairs.

Notwithstanding his qualifications, Crocker underwent a bitter and protracted confirmation struggle when nominated by President Reagan. Senator Jesse Helms (R–North Carolina), on the right, charged that he was not a true Reagan conservative but rather a regional specialist who would be overly sympathetic to black Africa. At the same time, Crocker was criticized from the left for leaning toward Pretoria, an allegation that followed the disclosure of classified documents summarizing talks between Crocker and South African officials that were leaked to TransAfrica, a black lobbying organization on African and Caribbean issues. (See Appendix A.)

Following his confirmation, Crocker moved quickly to establish bureaucratic control, gaining the confidence of Secretaries of State Alexander Haig and, later, George Shultz. Given virtually a free hand in southern African affairs during the first four years of the Reagan administration, Crocker set a precedent for influence and survival in office. He served longer than any other State Department official in charge of a regional bureau during the Reagan administration and was the longest-serving assistant secretary of state for African affairs since the bureau was created in 1958. It was not until Reagan's second term, when the sanctions debate became heated, that officials within the administration challenged Crocker's grip on policy. However, during Reagan's last year in office he reasserted his influence as the driving force behind the protracted but ultimately successful Angolan and Namibian negotiations.

The Genesis of Constructive Engagement

Crocker spelled out the essence of constructive engagement in an article published in *Foreign Affairs* in late 1980 and in other pieces timed for the presidential election of that year. He had written extensively during the Carter period, faulting policymakers principally for their failure to understand South African politics and the insecurities of the white minority population.

Some observers viewed his ideas as a conceptual throwback to the 1970s, when Henry Kissinger, during the Nixon administration, pursued a policy of "communication" with the South African government stressing mutual strategic and commercial interests. "Once again," wrote William Lewis, "the African continent is at the center of globalist planning and our political-military needs."[1] It is true that superpower rivalry exerted a major influence on constructive engagement. Crocker himself, in one of his early meetings with the South Africans, declared that the top U.S. priority was to stop Soviet encroachment in Africa.[2] But his policy was far more nuanced and ambitious than previous Republican policies. Six months before

Reagan's election, Crocker wrote that it was too late to revive Kissinger's approach: "There can be no turning back of the clock in U.S.–South African relations."[3]

Constructive engagement, he implied, was a new beginning. It was "neither the clandestine embrace" of the Nixon administration nor "the polecat treatment" of the Carter years.[4] Crocker was convinced that a number of factors combined to create an unprecedented opportunity for U.S. diplomacy in South Africa and the region. He believed that the South African government, under the leadership of Pieter W. Botha, had become a "modernizing autocracy" committed to reform; that most of the states in the region were in "pragmatic hands"; that the "conflicts in Namibia and Angola [were] tantalizingly close to some resolution";[5] and that the election of President Reagan had given the United States new credibility with Pretoria because of "our mandate and our desire to turn a new leaf in bilateral relations."[6]

Crocker indicated that a new relationship, based on the political reality within South Africa, could be established between South Africa and the United States. "The Botha government," he wrote, "has committed itself to a moderate reformist process whose ultimate end remains utterly unclear. . . . The current fluidity does not make meaningful change certain, but it does make it possible."[7] Crocker believed that Botha's first tentative reforms might encourage the government to consider more profound changes. And even if that did not occur, the reforms would have unintended consequences that would lead to wider black political participation.

Crocker wrote that Botha had carried out the Afrikaner equivalent of "a drawn-out coup d'etat" in which he was building up a solid coalition of like-minded "modernizers" who were "pragmatic, flexible, determined" rather than ideological. He saw the South African military, which had gained increased political influence under P. W. Botha, as "a lobby of modernizing patriots," and argued that "it would be unwise to view the South African Defense Force as an instrument of domestic brutality or as the rogue elephant of southern Africa, crashing across borders and wrecking Western interests."[8]

The United States could best promote change in South Africa, according to Crocker, by working with the white power structure and taking account of white fears. "Our objective," he said, "is to increase the South African government's confidence."[9] Serving as a broker in the resolution of regional disputes should therefore be a critical part of U.S. strategy. Regional security would diminish white South Africans' siege mentality, produced by their country's isolation in the region, and increase their willingness to embark on a program of serious reform. Based on this premise, external pressures, such as public criticism and sanctions, would be counterproductive, exacerbate white fears, and increase government intransigence.

But Crocker warned against South African manipulation, specifically the danger that the South Africans might try to use their relationship with the United States "as a smokescreen for other actions and misadventures with their neighbors." While underscoring the Soviet threat, Crocker rejected the South African notion of a "total onslaught" by the Soviet Union against South Africa. He made it clear that "in Africa we distinguish between countries where Soviets and Cubans have a combat presence, and those where governments [espouse] Marxism for their own practical purposes."[10]

This was a critical distinction that later came to be important in accounting for different U.S. policies toward Angola and Mozambique. Crocker told South African officials that he agreed with the African view that the South African government contributed to instability in the region when the latter went "beyond reprisal" in cross-border attacks against its neighbors.[11] However, on balance, Crocker stressed the similarities rather than the differences between Washington and Pretoria. He felt that the Reagan administration offered South Africa the "best shot" at improving relations and that the administration's credibility was on the line in making this new approach work.

Crocker did not devote comparable attention to black South African politics in his writings or to ways in which the United States could support black political aspirations. He wrote that "we need to know more about black attitudes, organization strategies and bargaining power," and described "the black political arena" as "an increasingly complex puzzle for outsiders."[12]

Finally, Crocker sounded a warning note on U.S. leverage. The United States had "limited influence" over the South African government, which should be "carefully husbanded for specific application to concrete issues of change." And if that meant the United States "becomes engaged in what some observers label as only 'amelioration,' so be it, provided that the process is open-ended and consistent with a non-racial order." Advocating a "nimble and sustained" U.S. diplomacy, Crocker ended his assessment on a realistic note: "As in other foreign policy agendas for the 1980s, the motto should be: underpromise and overdeliver—for a change."[13]

———

As Crocker's strategy evolved, it became evident that it rested on other important assumptions. The report of the Secretary of State's Advisory Committee, a high-level bipartisan group created by President Reagan's executive order of September 1985 to examine the policy after it ran into trouble, listed four interrelated premises at the core of constructive engagement:

> First, South Africa's overwhelming economic and military predominance in southern Africa and its powerful internal security apparatus would, at least in the short term, enable Pretoria to "manage" internal and external pressures for change. Second, the Botha government could be induced to agree to an internationally accepted settlement in Namibia if South African withdrawal were linked to a withdrawal of Cuban troops from Angola and the prospect of an improvement in U.S.–South African relations. Third, an early Namibian settlement would set in motion a self-reinforcing spiral of positive developments in South Africa and the region, thus validating the constructive engagement approach. Fourth, progress could be made more quickly on apartheid issues if the U.S. government used official rather than public channels for its criticism and pressure.[14]

In order to set the tone of the new policy, the Reagan administration began its tenure by sending a number of positive signals to Pretoria. In March 1981, only two months after Reagan assumed the presidency, South African military officials, including high-level intelligence officers, arrived in Washington to consult with U.S. officials. Although the White House stated that the South Africans had obtained their visas fraudulently by posing as Foreign Ministry officials and hiding their military associations, the event signaled the start of closer working relations between Pretoria and Washington. The administration authorized more South African honorary consuls in the United States, granted visas to a South African rugby team, reestablished military attachés in both capitals, relaxed controls on nonlethal exports that could be used by the South African military and police, and adopted a more flexible attitude toward the sale of dual-use military equipment and sophisticated technology. Cumulatively, these measures, though small in themselves, sent an unmistakable message of closer cooperation between the United States and South Africa.

The administration also stated its opposition to apartheid, but without the consistency or conviction of the Carter administration. Instead, the Reagan administration limited its public criticism and offered cautious praise for Pretoria's reforms. For example, when a whites-only referendum in November 1983 approved a new constitution granting limited parliamentary participation to Coloureds and Indians but excluding the majority African population, the State Department quickly gave it a qualified endorsement. Even though the new constitution was widely opposed by both black and white anti-apartheid forces in South Africa, the administration described it as a "step in the right direction."

While sensitive to white South African attitudes, Crocker was less responsive to blacks and was perceived as such by blacks in South Africa, many of whom believed that the United States had become a close ally of the South African government. In addition to endorsing a constitution that excluded Africans, Crocker did not meet with many black leaders, nor did he address their political concerns in his speeches. William Finnegan, writing in *Mother Jones,* reported that when Herman Nickel, the U.S. ambassador to South Africa, was asked about his embassy's lack of contact with blacks, he suggested that this "had become policy, that too much contact with the government's opponents in the townships might endanger the delicate negotiations over Namibia."[15]

The Southern Africa Region

At the outset, constructive engagement was presented primarily as a strategy for achieving political change within South Africa. But in practice, Crocker, like his predecessors, concentrated on regional concerns.

The United States first became involved in southern Africa when Henry Kissinger launched a major initiative in 1976. Following the war in Vietnam, Kissinger was worried about the growth of Soviet influence in other volatile parts of the world. In southern Africa, Angola was the focus of this concern. After the withdrawal of the Portuguese from the country in 1975 as the result of a coup in Lisbon the year before, a three-sided civil war broke out that quickly drew in powerful outsiders. The United States provided covert aid to the two parties it considered pro-Western, the Front for the National Liberation of Angola (FNLA) and the Union for the Total Independence of Angola (UNITA). South Africa also supported these groups by sending in troops to help them fight against the Popular Movement for the Liberation of Angola (MPLA), a self-styled Marxist party that turned to the Eastern bloc for assistance.

The Soviet Union flew in thousands of Cuban troops and dispatched large amounts of arms to strengthen the MPLA. Key African states that had remained neutral, such as Nigeria, and some European countries reacted to the South African intervention by recognizing the MPLA as the government of Angola. In early 1976, fearing another Vietnam-like entanglement and wanting to distance the United States from South Africa's actions, Congress enacted the Clark Amendment, sponsored by Senator Dick Clark (D–Iowa), which prohibited aid to any of the warring groups in Angola. South Africa withdrew its forces and the MPLA consolidated its power over much of the country.

Having failed to check Soviet and Cuban influence in Angola, Kissinger turned his attention to ending white minority rule in Rhodesia in order to forestall further Soviet inroads in the region. He was unsuccessful in removing Ian Smith, the leader of the government and the architect of the country's white settler rebellion against Britain's colonial rule. However, he obtained Smith's agreement to the principle of majority rule and, in the process, launched a negotiating sequence adopted by future administrations that put Rhodesia first, Namibia second, and South Africa last in U.S. policy priorities.

Although the Carter administration placed greater stress on human rights than Kissinger had done, it shared his concern about the Cuban military presence in Angola and withheld recognition of the Angolan government. However, for the most part, the Carter administration set the Angolan situation aside. Instead, it concentrated on using multilateral diplomacy to bring majority rule and independence to Rhodesia and Namibia. In addition, the Carter administration was much more openly critical of South Africa than its predecessors had been.

Notwithstanding differences in emphasis, there was continuity between Kissinger and the Carter administration in the broad policy goals of strengthening U.S. influence in the region, reducing Soviet-bloc involvement, and establishing regional stability. These were also the goals of Chester Crocker. His strategic and tactical reasoning, however, was different. He disapproved of strong public criticism and multilateral diplomatic overtures that put Pretoria on the defensive. He believed that the best way to enlist South Africa's cooperation was to use inducements rather than pressure. Furthermore, he concluded that the removal of the 20,000 Cuban troops from Angola would allay South Africa's security fears about Communist encroachment in the region. A Cuban withdrawal, he reasoned, would also permit the United States to extend its influence in Angola and normalize relations with the MPLA government, a step that had been taken by most of the international community but rejected by successive U.S. administrations.

The South African government eagerly entered into discussions of regional problems with the Reagan administration. Its main concerns were the military threats posed by two black nationalist movements—the South-West African People's Organization (SWAPO), which was fighting for independence in Namibia, and the African National Congress (ANC), which was fighting to end white rule in South Africa itself. South African officials made it clear that they were especially concerned about the prospect of SWAPO winning UN-supervised elections and taking over the government in Namibia. At that time, the Cuban presence in Angola seemed to be low on Pretoria's security agenda. The South Africans, for example, barely mentioned it in their early talks with the United States over Namibia.[16]

However, while these exploratory talks were going on, Pretoria adopted a more aggressive posture in the region, especially against Angola and Mozambique. Its intention, the *Economist* later observed, was "to create 'a shield of instability' to deter incursion [of the ANC and SWAPO guerrillas]" and to buy time to push ahead with domestic reform.[17] South Africa's destabilization policy, as its military and other punitive pressures against its neighbors came to be known, steadily escalated in the 1980s to include cross-border raids; assassinations; letter and car bomb attacks; support for dissident movements in Angola, Mozambique, Zimbabwe, and Lesotho; and economic and political pressures of various kinds. Just as constructive engagement was being launched, therefore, Pretoria was stepping up its aggressive attacks against its neighbors.

The convergence of these two dynamics—Crocker's stabilizing diplomacy and Pretoria's destabilizing militancy—were to have serious consequences for U.S. diplomacy and the strategy of constructive engagement. The contradiction, however, did not shake Crocker's conviction that the best way to obtain the South African government's cooperation was to stress the two countries' common strategic interests in the region. This became apparent in his marathon diplomatic efforts to achieve a joint settlement in Angola and Namibia, an issue that absorbed the bulk of Crocker's attention and much of the energy of the State Department's Africa Bureau during the eight years of the Reagan administration.

Namibia/Angola. The Carter administration had made a major effort to secure the independence of Namibia (South-West Africa), a former German colony roughly twice the size of Texas with a population of just over a million people. The territory had been controlled by South Africa since the end of World War I. The South African government regarded Namibia as a protective buffer zone against the surrounding black states and repeatedly rejected calls by the United Nations and the international community for its independence.

SWAPO, the main Namibian nationalist movement, had been waging a low-intensity guerrilla war against South Africa since 1966. The insurgency intensified when Angola became independent in 1975 and the MPLA government in Luanda allowed SWAPO to establish bases in the south of the country and launch raids across the Namibian border. On the international front, the Carter administration took the initiative in 1977 by organizing a "contact group" consisting of five Western nations—the United Kingdom, France, West Germany, Canada, and the United States itself—that developed a plan calling for a cease-fire between SWAPO and South African forces, UN-supervised elections, and Namibia's independence. The proposal, which involved negotiations with South Africa and SWAPO and was agreed to by them, was adopted by the UN Security Council as Resolution 435 in September 1978.

After protracted discussions about implementing the UN plan, South Africa balked during a conference of the major parties in Geneva in January 1981, saying that implementation was "premature." The approaching inauguration of President Reagan appeared to offer the South Africans the possibility of a better deal. Pretoria was also concerned about the likelihood of SWAPO, in a free election, defeating the Namibian parties that were under South Africa's influence. Further, political considerations within South Africa played a role in the government's decision. Prime Minister (later President) P. W. Botha was facing his first national election as the leader of the ruling National Party and feared that his rightwing opposition might make political capital out of what it would regard as a "sell-out" in Namibia.

The Reagan administration endorsed the UN plan for Namibia's independence but modified the approach for achieving its implementation in two important ways. First, it dealt directly with South Africa, bypassing the Western contact group; and second, it created a more complex diplomatic package by linking Namibia's independence with the withdrawal of Cuban troops from Angola. Linkage was not an entirely new concept. The Carter administration had recognized the relationship between the two issues but had not made progress on one dependent on progress on the other. Its view was that once Namibia became independent, Angola would no longer feel threatened by the presence on its southern border of South African forces that made periodic cross-border attacks. With the South African threat removed, Angola could be expected to fulfill its publicly stated promise to send the Cubans home.

By contrast, Crocker saw Namibian independence and Cuban withdrawal as "empirically" connected objectives that had to be formally linked at the negotiating table. His approach was consistent with constructive engagement in that it offered an opportunity to establish a better relationship with the South African government and stressed the notion that the United States shared Pretoria's concerns about Soviet-bloc influence in the region.

The concept of linkage was first presented at a meeting in Cape Town in June 1981 between South African officials and a U.S. delegation consisting of Crocker, Deputy Secretary of State William P. Clark (who six months later became national security adviser), and Assistant Secretary of State for Human Rights Elliott Abrams (who later became assistant secretary of state for Inter-American affairs). At that time, reported the *New York Times,* there was "a meeting of minds between Pretoria and Washington" when the United States proposed a quid pro quo: If the United States would get the Cubans out of Angola, then South Africa would implement the UN plan for Namibia's independence. The South Africans formally agreed to the proposal shortly afterward.

The formula struck a responsive chord in South Africa for three principal reasons. First, by making South Africa's withdrawal from Namibia conditional on a Cuban withdrawal from Angola, linkage increased the number of players involved, thus diffusing responsibility for a settlement. Second, it allowed Pretoria to exert more control over the process. The South African military had often crossed the Angolan border to attack SWAPO bases and help UNITA. These incursions made it difficult for the Luanda government to dispense with the Cubans. By continuing these forays, South Africa could ensure that the Cubans remained, shifting the onus for delaying Namibia's independence onto the Angolans and the Americans.

Third, by elevating the importance of the Cubans, linkage lent credibility to the South African military's doctrine of "total on-slaught." This doctrine held that the South African government was a target of a Moscow-directed offensive aimed at replacing it with a pliant Communist regime.

For Crocker, linkage was politically advantageous because it stressed the East-West conflict, an ideological outlook that appealed to those conservatives who had opposed his nomination. The *Wall Street Journal* commented, "Chester Crocker, the U.S. Assistant Secretary of State who is point man in the negotiations, has played a brilliant diplomatic game so far. . . . By tying Cuban withdrawal from Angola to a Namibian settlement, he has overcome South African intransigence and shifted the spotlight of public opinion to Cuban and Russian imperialism." Crocker also believed that successful implementation of linkage would have a beneficial ripple effect throughout Africa. It would bring freedom to Namibia, the last of Africa's white-ruled states except for South Africa itself; permit the opening of formal diplomatic relations with Angola; and facilitate closer U.S. ties with other African states.

Initially, the new approach seemed to make headway. Bilateral talks between Pretoria and Washington resolved a number of outstanding technical issues in the UN plan, including the election formula, the monitoring of guerrilla bases, the composition of the international peacekeeping forces, and various logistical problems. In July 1982, a year after the Cape Town meeting, the *New York Times* reported that Pretoria had dropped "virtually every one of the procedural demands and quibbles that had been thrown in the face of the Carter administration to forestall a settlement."

Crocker appeared confident that, once the South Africans were satisfied, the Angolans would be brought in and the package quickly put together. U.S. officials indicated that an agreement was imminent and that the UN plan would be implemented by late summer or early fall, with Namibian elections seven months later. A State Department official remarked that "nothing left on Namibia could be defined as a serious enough issue to jeopardize the negotiations."[18]

Still, the larger political questions remained unresolved. Given South Africa's continuing attacks on Angola, what was not clear was how the Reagan administration would fulfill its part of the linkage arrangement by persuading Angola to send the Cubans home. Nor was it clear how the Cubans, the Soviets, or UNITA would respond. There was also concern in Washington about South Africa's motives. Most troubling was the apparent contradiction between South Africa's seeming readiness to resolve specific issues in the UN plan and its escalating military activities in Namibia and Angola.

South Africa's first military involvement in Angola was in the 1960s, when it supported the Portuguese in their struggle with a growing black insurgency. Then came the ill-fated intervention in 1975–76, when South Africa tried to influence the tripartite struggle for control of Angola's newly independent government. Of the two parties that South Africa had supported, the FNLA—which had also been supported by the United States—disintegrated, leaving UNITA, led by Jonas Savimbi, as the MPLA government's remaining opponent. South Africa then concentrated on reequipping and retraining UNITA, whose political power base was in southeastern Angola, near the Namibian border.

South African forces often crossed the Angolan border, ostensibly to destroy SWAPO bases in southern Angola but increasingly to help UNITA. An extensive assault in 1979 was followed by an even larger one in 1981, Operation Protea, which involved 5,000 South African troops who met relatively little resistance. Another major incursion, Operation Askari, took place in 1983, but this time Angolan forces—armed by the Soviets with more weaponry and backed by Cuban troops—resisted more effectively. By 1984 South Africa had established an occupied area inside Angola's southern border, UNITA was expanding its operations in a widening arc across the country, the civil war was wreaking enormous human and economic destruction, and the MPLA government had become more dependent than ever on its Cuban and Soviet allies.

During this period, Crocker concentrated on securing South Africa's compliance by refraining from publicly criticizing Pretoria and by protecting it in the United Nations. He made it clear that the Reagan administration sympathized with Pretoria's claim that it had a right to defend itself against SWAPO's attacks, even if this meant crossing international borders. In August 1981 the United States cast the only vote against a UN Security Council resolution condemning South Africa's invasion of Angola. Crocker assumed that the cooperation of the Angolans would be obtained "once they are made to realize that they can only get a Namibian settlement through us." They would have to come around, he privately assured skeptics, because they would see that "this was the only game in town."[19]

In this atmosphere, one deadline after another passed without progress on either the Cuban troop withdrawal or Namibia's independence. By 1983 the United States was seeking a cease-fire between the Angolan army and the joint UNITA–South African forces as an interim step; and in February 1984 it facilitated an agreement between Pretoria and Luanda known as the Lusaka Agreement. The text was never published, but press reports stated that it called for the disengagement of South African and Angolan forces in southern Angola and the establishment of a joint South African–Angolan team to supervise the withdrawal of Pretoria's troops. The agreement also reportedly required Angola to restrain SWAPO guerrillas from attacking Namibia.

Initially the pact seemed to work, with joint South African–Angolan military patrols monitoring the war zone. However, South Africa's withdrawal proceeded more slowly than anticipated, and the

Lusaka Agreement achieved only a temporary lull in the hostilities. By the end of Reagan's first term, fighting resumed, the Cuban forces in Angola had increased substantially—up from 20,000 to approximately 35,000—and the prospects for a South African withdrawal from Namibia seemed more remote than ever.

Mozambique and Zimbabwe. South Africa's destabilization tactics against its neighbors went far beyond what Crocker had originally regarded as defensive and deterrent responses to SWAPO and ANC guerrilla infiltration. Pretoria's military incursions were threatening the survival of individual governments and the stability of the region as a whole—a situation, in Washington's view, that would open up new opportunities for Soviet interference. This concern, plus frustration at the slow pace of negotiations over Namibia and Angola, encouraged the administration to pay closer attention to other critical countries in the region, notably Mozambique and Zimbabwe.

Mozambique was the more vulnerable of the two. The Mozambique Liberation Front (FRELIMO), a nationalist movement organized on Marxist lines that came to power after Mozambique's independence from Portugal in 1975, inherited one of the world's poorest countries. It quickly became embroiled in regional hostilities when it allowed guerrillas fighting for majority rule in Rhodesia to use its territory as a base for attacks against the white minority government. Nevertheless, FRELIMO managed to avoid confrontation with South Africa during the early years of independence, when South African Prime Minister John Vorster pursued a policy of dialogue with Africa. The accession of P. W. Botha to the South African leadership in 1978, however, and the expanded use of Mozambique as a launching pad for ANC guerrilla attacks against South Africa produced a marked change in the relationship between the two countries.

By the early 1980s, Mozambique had become a major target of South Africa's destabilization policy. The country, which shared a border with South Africa, was not only a base for ANC operations but also played a pivotal role in the region as the main trade outlet to the sea for several of the independent black states. However, South Africa did not directly attack the FRELIMO government. Pretoria's principal instrument of destabilization was the Mozambique National Resistance (RENAMO), a little-known insurgent group that had been set up by Rhodesian intelligence in the mid-1970s to weaken Mozambique's ability to support anti-Rhodesian guerrilla forces. Just before Rhodesia (now Zimbabwe) became independent in April 1980, it handed RENAMO over to South Africa "lock, stock, and barrel," in the words of the then head of Rhodesian intelligence.[20]

Pretoria rebuilt this disintegrating group of former Portuguese security officers, demobilized Mozambican soldiers, and FRELIMO deserters into a ruthless hit-and-run force that destroyed the rural economy, attacked civilians—often committing brutal atrocities—and seriously undermined the FRELIMO government. RENAMO, like UNITA, flourished under South Africa's patronage, but it differed from the Angolan movement in several important respects. RENAMO had no indigenous origin; it also lacked clear leadership, a coherent political philosophy, and legitimacy as a nationalist movement.

Mozambique had close political ties with the Soviet Union, which had supported FRELIMO's anticolonial war. Shortly after Mozambique's independence in 1975, the two countries signed a treaty of friendship and cooperation, and the Soviet Union and its allies supplied large amounts of military aid and technical assistance in the early 1980s. Nonetheless, the country's internal situation continued to deteriorate. RENAMO expanded its operations, a long drought and other natural disasters caused widespread famine that was exacerbated by the insurgency, and FRELIMO's doctrinaire socialist policies proved to be flawed. All these factors contributed to the collapse of the economy and to a general social deterioration. As a result, Maputo began to turn to the West for assistance, to gradually retreat from its socialist dogma, and to consider closer cooperation with Pretoria on security and economic issues.

The Reagan administration's relations with Mozambique started badly, with Maputo expelling four U.S. diplomats accused of spying in 1981. The United States accused Cuba, which had approximately six hundred military advisers in Mozambique, of instigating the expulsion and retaliated by suspending food aid and downgrading diplomatic relations.

Nevertheless, after a cooling-off period, relations slowly improved. Crocker responded to the FRELIMO government's desire to reach out to the West and took a more sympathetic view of Mozambique's security predicament. With his persistent encouragement, the Mozambican government began cautious negotiations with South Africa. These led in March 1984 to the signing of the Nkomati Accord, "a nonaggression and good neighborliness" pact between the two countries. The agreement was wider in scope than the Lusaka Agreement, which had been signed a month earlier between South Africa and Angola. Under the Nkomati Accord, South Africa agreed to discontinue its assistance to RENAMO. For

Mozambique, the accord involved curtailing the ANC's activities inside the country and preventing it from using Mozambique as a base or transit route for guerrilla operations against South Africa.

While Mozambique adhered to its part of the bargain, South Africa continued to send military supplies to RENAMO. On one occasion, fifteen months after the signing of the accord, Louis Nel, South Africa's deputy foreign minister, flew secretly to Mozambique to meet a RENAMO leader.[21] Nevertheless, the United States encouraged Mozambique to adhere to the pact, and Washington's relations with Mozambique continued to improve. U.S. economic aid was resumed, and in September 1984, Mozambican President Samora Machel was welcomed at the White House. After Machel's death in a plane crash just inside South Africa near the Mozambique border in October 1986, his successor, Joaquim Chissano, continued to seek Western economic and military support and encourage friendly relations with the United States.

In his efforts to strengthen U.S. influence in the region, Crocker continued the Carter administration's policy of support for Zimbabwe. Becoming independent in 1980, only nine months before Reagan took office, Zimbabwe was important for several reasons. Centrally located and sharing a border with South Africa, the country was the most economically developed of the black states in southern Africa. Its leader, Robert Mugabe, who had come to power in British-run elections following a long civil war with Ian Smith's white minority government, was a self-avowed Marxist and a strong critic of apartheid. Yet his relations with the Soviet Union were not friendly. Moscow had backed Joshua Nkomo, Mugabe's wartime ally but subsequent rival; China had supported Mugabe.

Following independence, Mugabe pursued a policy of racial reconciliation, fostered a mixed economy, established cordial diplomatic relations with the West, and notwithstanding his political ideology and his opposition to Pretoria, developed a working understanding with South Africa on security and trade matters. He gave full political and diplomatic support to the ANC, but refused to allow ANC guerrillas to establish bases in Zimbabwe or travel through the country to launch attacks against South Africa.

Crocker believed, unlike many conservatives in the United States, that Mugabe's government should be helped and strengthened. Accordingly, building on the foundation of support for Zimbabwe established by the Carter administration, a U.S. aid package of $225 million over a three-year period was authorized in FY 1981.

Further, when Zimbabwe became a target of South Africa's sporadic but debilitating economic harassment—due to Mugabe's hostile rhetoric rather than any aggressive actions—Crocker interceded with Pretoria, with some success.

The administration's assumption seemed to be that Mugabe's pragmatism and nonalignment would ensure continuing good relations. By the mid-1980s, however, bilateral ties had deteriorated. The downturn was a result of a series of events: (1) Zimbabwe's harsh crackdown on dissidents who supported Nkomo; (2) anti-U.S. votes by Zimbabwe in the United Nations on the Korean Air Lines flight shot down by the USSR and the American invasion of Grenada; (3) a strained visit by Mugabe to the United States in 1983, during which he rigidly defended these actions and made the tactical error of lecturing President Reagan during their only meeting; and (4) concerns by American conservatives about socialism and the movement toward a one-party state.

Finally, in July 1986, an anti-U.S. speech by a Zimbabwean junior minister during an American Independence Day celebration in Harare, attended by former President Jimmy Carter, brought matters to a head. The United States ended its bilateral aid program, announcing the decision in August 1986 just as Mugabe was playing host to leaders of the 101-member Non-Aligned Movement. After a two-year hiatus, during which tempers cooled and Mugabe and Nkomo reconciled their differences, U.S. aid was resumed, albeit at a greatly reduced level, with the announcement in September 1988 of a $17-million two-year grant to stimulate development and business activity in Zimbabwe.

The Domestic Dimension

At home, Crocker's policy generated cautious optimism during much of Reagan's first term. The administration justified its cordial relationship with Pretoria by citing progress on Namibia. Several procedural problems in the UN plan for Namibia's independence were resolved, and the administration reported that it was making progress in negotiations with South Africa and the Angolan government. Many foreign policy analysts gave the administration the benefit of the doubt, concluding that constructive engagement had possibilities and should be given a chance.

Congressional skeptics, however, expressed concern that the administration's heavy emphasis on the Namibian/Angolan issue and on gaining the trust of Pretoria gave the impression that Washington was disregarding the question of black political rights within South Africa. In a speech to the American Legion in Honolulu in August 1981, shortly after he was sworn in, Crocker appeared to weaken the traditional U.S. anti-apartheid stance. "In South Africa, the region's dominant country," he said, "it is not our task to choose between black and white."

The Reagan administration did, however, provide educational and development aid to black South Africans as part of a wider effort that later became known as "black empowerment." The first such initiatives had come in the 1970s from religious institutions, foundations, and the business sector. On the government side, Congress led the way. In 1980 a bipartisan move organized by Stephen Solarz (D–New York), chairman of the House of Representatives Subcommittee on Africa, resulted in the authorization of a two-year scholarship program for black South Africans. Totaling $8 million, the program, as with all U.S. foreign assistance, was to be administered by the U.S. Agency for International Development (USAID). While implementation was delayed by bureaucratic and administrative problems, the Carter administration, during its last year in office, had made a gesture of support for Congress's initiative by offering a scholarship grant of $38,000.

The Reagan administration's first allocation of $40,000 was made in FY 1981. The USAID program got seriously underway in FY 1982, when $4 million from the Solarz package was disbursed. In FY 1983, toward the end of Reagan's first term, the aid figure rose to $10 million, and the program was broadened beyond education to cover a range of human rights and development activities. The level dropped to $5 million in FY 1984, before rising to $8 million in FY 1985, $19 million in FY 1986, $20 million in FY 1987, and $25 million in FY 1988. The major increases in 1983, 1985, and 1986 occurred during times of heightened congressional pressure for sanctions.

Originally, the Reagan administration justified aid to black South Africans on humanitarian grounds. In fact, before coming to office, Crocker had advocated improving the living conditions of blacks, stressing education as a priority and chastising Western governments and educational institutions for not doing enough. In later years, a more overtly political rationale was cited by the administration. The "central thrust" of the program, said John C. Whitehead, deputy secretary of state, was to enhance "the economic power of blacks . . . vis-à-vis South Africa's governing elite," and "to help turn it to political advantage."[22]

Throughout, the Reagan administration believed that aid to South African blacks was a politically acceptable alternative to sanctions. Alan Keyes, who first worked in the State Department's Policy Planning Bureau and later served under Jeane Kirkpatrick in the U.S. delegation to the United Nations, was one of the most prominent exponents of this view. A black American with a conservative perspective, Keyes was widely credited with having coined the term "black empowerment."

Although the aid program enjoyed bipartisan support in Congress throughout the 1980s, there was a behind-the-scenes struggle between the House and Senate staffs during its formative years. The controversy was not over the principle of aid to black South Africans or the level of funding. Rather, the debate turned on what kinds of projects and organizations should be supported. The House Subcommittee on Africa put a hold on those USAID projects it felt were white dominated or not considered "credible" by the black community. "We wanted to send a political message, to show that we cared about the anti-apartheid movement, to help anti-apartheid leaders build a base for a post-apartheid society," said Stephen Weissman, staff director of the House Subcommittee on Africa. "This involved directing aid to groups promoting alternative models of education, for example, not to state schools."[23]

The alternative view, presented by Philip L. Christenson, former professional staff member of the Senate Foreign Relations Committee and later aide to Senator Helms, was that the program should focus on educational projects carried out by established institutions, even if they were controlled and financed by the South African government. The types of projects advanced by the House subcommittee, he argued, were "not consistent with constructive engagement" because they strengthened antigovernment organizations "run by political activists."[24]

Crocker and other senior administration officials were only marginally involved in this debate. USAID broadly accepted the criteria set forth by the House, funding nonracial, grassroots projects that had no connection with the South African government.[25] As a consequence, the $91 million in aid that went to black South Africans during the Reagan administration covered a wide range of activities, including privately sponsored educational and training programs, community outreach, legal assistance, leadership development, black businesses, and training for labor leaders.

In addition to Crocker, President Reagan and others also played a large part in shaping the public's perception of the administration's policy toward South Africa. President Carter, a southern liberal, believed that the United States had to stand for racial equality and human rights in South Africa. In contrast, Reagan, an ideological conservative, felt that the United States had to oppose communism and protect its strategic interests in the region. His remarks were invariably cast in this context.

Unlike his predecessor, Reagan showed little interest in the apartheid issue until domestic political pressures forced him to take a public stand. When he did allude to South Africa, it seemed clear that his sympathies were with the white government and were often based on inaccurate information. For instance, he frequently referred to the support South Africa had given the Allies in World War II, missing the fact that South Africa's ruling National Party, which was not in power at the time, had been sympathetic to Nazi Germany and opposed fighting on the side of the Allies.

In an interview with Walter Cronkite on March 3, 1981, the president portrayed South Africa as a historical friend, asking: "Can we abandon a country that has stood by us in every war we've ever fought, a country that strategically is essential to the free world in its production of minerals we all must have and so forth?" A day later, President Botha responded: "It is good to know that the leader of the free world acknowledges and appreciates the strategic importance of South Africa. We welcome this greater understanding of and greater realism toward South Africa."

When referring to the widespread unrest that erupted in South Africa in 1984, Reagan often downplayed the country's racial injustice and misleadingly attributed the turmoil to tribalism. During a radio interview on August 24, 1985, he argued that South Africa had "eliminated the segregation we once had in our own country." At a meeting with newspaper editors and broadcasters in June 1986, he stated: "What we're seeing now is an outright civil war that is going on, and it's no longer just a contest between the black population and the white population. It is blacks fighting blacks, because there's still a tribal situation involved there in that community."

While Crocker's preeminence tended to obscure the role of other members of his team in the State Department's Africa Bureau, two individuals from the early years deserve mention. The first, Frank Wisner, a career foreign service officer who had been ambassador to Zambia and was Crocker's senior deputy in Reagan's first term, helped to mollify criticism of the policy by becoming the administration's "point man" with the Africans. As gregarious as Crocker was reserved, Wisner, who subsequently became ambassador to Egypt, took an active part in attempts to allay African suspicions of constructive engagement.

The second, Herman Nickel, was Crocker's personal choice for ambassador to South Africa in Reagan's first term. Nickel was a former journalist for *Time* and *Fortune* magazines and was strongly opposed to sanctions. During his tour, which ended in 1986, he became a target of critics who felt that constructive engagement had aligned the United States too closely with the South African government. South African blacks as well as American critics complained that he maintained a closer relationship with South Africa's white community than either diplomacy or the political realities of the situation demanded.

By the end of 1982, criticism of constructive engagement was growing. The perception in Congress and in Africa was that the policy had failed to achieve its immediate objective of a Namibian settlement and was tacitly encouraging South Africa's destabilization of its neighbors. Most important, it seemed to have had no impact on the Botha government's position on political rights for blacks. In November 1982 Vice President George Bush was sent on a tour of African countries to explain his government's policies. But Congress was of even greater concern to the administration. A number of bills and resolutions condemning South Africa and U.S. policy and urging varying degrees of sanctions reflected slowly mounting congressional opposition.

In response to the criticism, Under Secretary of State Lawrence Eagleburger delivered a speech in June 1983 laying out the full regional scope of the policy and criticizing apartheid in the strongest language the administration had used since taking office. Angolan-Namibian linkage was played down, and UNITA, which the administration had often described as a "legitimate political force" in Angola, was not mentioned. Instead, a third of the speech was devoted to internal events in South Africa.

For the first time, the administration stated in some detail its support of "those inside and outside government in South Africa who are committed to peaceful change." The homelands, bannings, removals, and detentions were all condemned. "The political system is morally wrong," Eagleburger said. He emphasized the growing direct U.S. financial aid for black South Africans, but rejected U.S. disinvestment and all forms of economic pressure. The clear tone of the speech became ambiguous, however, when Eagleburger discussed Botha's reforms: "We recognize the limits of current change and do not make a practice of endorsing individual steps. . . . at the same time . . . it is incumbent on us to avoid the arrogance of rejecting such steps."

Despite the growing skepticism, Crocker managed to keep doubts about his policy in check during Reagan's first term. Indeed, the first half of 1984 marked a high point for constructive engagement. While a Namibian settlement, Crocker's prime objective, still proved elusive, there were other noteworthy developments. The Lusaka Agreement between South Africa and Angola and the Nkomati Accord between South Africa and Mozambique, even though they later unraveled, demonstrated that the Reagan administration had become an active mediator in the region. The victory for Botha's new constitution in the November 1983 referendum reflected strong white support for his reform strategy, which Crocker had cautiously endorsed.

However, events began to go awry in the latter part of 1984. On September 3, the day the new South African constitution went into effect, violent protests broke out in some of the country's African townships. These were triggered in part by long-simmering local issues such as rents and education; the overriding grievance, though, was the new constitution, which called for a tricameral, racially segregated Parliament that gave limited voice to Coloureds and Indians but excluded Africans. The unrest spread rapidly across South Africa, turning into a popular uprising of unprecedented scope, duration, and intensity. The security forces responded by opening fire on rampaging youths, occupying black townships and schools, detaining thousands of protesters, and clamping down on the press.

Suddenly, at the end of Reagan's first term, apartheid became a major political controversy in the United States. Nightly television network news programs showed unarmed black demonstrators being attacked by South African police and soldiers, mass public funerals, and "necklace" killings, in which gasoline-soaked tires were thrown around the necks of known or suspected black collaborators by angry protesters and set on fire.

Constructive engagement had little to show when, in this charged atmosphere, questions were raised about what U.S. policy had accomplished. The Lusaka Agreement and the Nkomati Accord began to disintegrate following reports that South Africa had not lived up to the agreements. Instead of withdrawing from Angola, Pretoria increased its aid to UNITA and continued to provide clandestine military supplies to RENAMO. The Namibia talks were at an impasse. Furthermore, Pretoria showed no signs of opening a dialogue with credible black South African leaders. In fact, the centerpiece of South Africa's reform program—the new constitution—had set off protests that plunged the country into a violent insurrection. As the crisis in South Africa swelled, Crocker, who had worked quietly and stayed out of the limelight during his first four years in office, was abruptly thrust into the political crossfire.

Defiant South African woman
(International Defense & Aid Fund for Southern Africa)

South African police attack peaceful student demonstrators
(International Defense & Aid Fund for Southern Africa)

Black township funeral
(International Defense & Aid Fund for Southern Africa)

Senator Lowell Weicker, Congressman Mervyn M. Dymally, Randall Robinson,
and others protest at South African embassy   *(Rick Reinhard/Impact Visuals)*

Reagan's Second Term: Constructive Engagement Under Fire

On November 21, 1984, during the Thanksgiving holidays, three black Americans—Randall Robinson, the executive director of TransAfrica; Walter Fauntroy, the District of Columbia's delegate to Congress; and Mary Frances Berry, a member of the U.S. Civil Rights Commission—were arrested in front of the South African embassy in Washington, D.C., during a peaceful demonstration against apartheid. Thus began the campaign of the Free South Africa Movement (FSAM), a loose coalition of organizations and individuals brought together by Robinson and other activists to protest apartheid and Reagan's policy of constructive engagement.

The FSAM organized a series of demonstrations, rallies, and lobbying activities across the United States that attracted major media attention and galvanized a broad array of church, student, labor, and civil rights groups. From 1984 until the enactment of sanctions legislation in October 1986, about six thousand people were arrested while picketing the South African embassy and consulates. Among the demonstrators were eighteen members of Congress, including Senator Lowell Weicker (R–Connecticut), reportedly the first senator in U.S. history to be arrested for an act of civil disobedience while in office, and Patricia Schroeder (D–Colorado), an eight-term member of the House of Representatives. Two years after the first embassy arrests, the FSAM—strengthened by media attention, black South African leaders' calls for sanctions, and growing public awareness of the issue—claimed success with the passage of the Comprehensive Anti-Apartheid Act of 1986 (CAAA), a decisive rejection of the policy of constructive engagement.

The Road to Sanctions

Several factors contributed to the public surge of interest in the South Africa issue. The most important were the black revolt in South Africa and the government's heavy-handed response. The turmoil was shown by the electronic and print media in almost daily reports over a period of fourteen months, from September 1984, when the black protests began, to November 1985, when television cameras were banned by the South African government. These images conveyed a sense of revolutionary upheaval, sensitized Americans to the violent nature of apartheid, and depicted the frustration of black South Africans over their lack of political rights and the social and economic inequities of apartheid.

Individuals played a key role in shaping American public opinion, focusing the debate not only on apartheid but on the American response. Jesse Jackson, in his 1984 presidential campaign, ensured that the issue of U.S. involvement in South Africa was raised during an election year. And Randall Robinson, an activist who had been lobbying for sanctions against South Africa for years, emerged as an articulate and effective organizer.

The award of the 1984 Nobel Peace Prize to Bishop Desmond Tutu, announced while he was in the United States, focused worldwide attention on the conflict and made the Anglican priest an international celebrity. A religious leader with a telegenic presence and an affable personality, Tutu called for economic pressure as the only nonviolent way the international community could help dismantle apartheid. "Tutu manifested to white America the black struggle in South Africa in non-threatening terms," wrote one commentator.[26] In a survey conducted by the Chicago Council on Foreign Relations in 1986, Tutu, who by then had been elevated to archbishop, was selected as the second most admired leader in the world, following Philippine President Corazon Aquino.

The U.S. Anti-Apartheid Movement. Public concern about conditions in South Africa was rapidly translated into political action by a nationwide network of grassroots activists who, for nearly a decade, had been exerting pressure at the state and local government levels for the sale, or "divestment," of stock in U.S. firms operating in South Africa. The main organizations were the New York-based American Committee on Africa (ACOA), founded in 1953; the Interfaith Center on Corporate Responsibility (ICCR), set up in 1971 in New York; the Washington Office on Africa (WOA), an offshoot of the ACOA formed in 1972; and the American Friends Service Committee (AFSC), a Philadelphia-based Quaker organization that started its Southern Africa Project in 1977. Finally, there was TransAfrica, a black lobbying organization concerned with African and Caribbean affairs. Founded in 1977 and based in Washington, TransAfrica broadened the activists' agenda from divestment to an attack on U.S. policy. By lobbying Congress to enact laws that would make apartheid more costly for the South African government, TransAfrica became the principal organization spearheading the drive for comprehensive, mandatory sanctions against South Africa.

Since the 1970s, these groups had made slow but steady gains. However, their impact increased significantly after 1984 as the public became more aware of the issue through extensive media coverage of the South African crisis. By mid-1985 divestment legislation had been passed in six states, with fourteen others considering similar measures. Twenty-three cities either had enacted or were considering divestment. According to a study by Mitchell Investment Management Company, Inc., a specialist in social investing, by 1986 South Africa-related investment restrictions of some sort affected institutional assets of more than $220 billion; these represented the pension or endowment funds of 19 states, 68 cities and counties, and 131 colleges and universities.

In Washington, the Congressional Black Caucus, founded in 1970 and consisting of twenty-one members of the House of Representatives, took the lead in channeling the wave of popular concern over South Africa into political action in Congress. Congressman Ronald V. Dellums (D–California) introduced legislation that proposed cutting virtually all U.S. economic ties to South Africa. The administration realized that its policy was threatened when the Dellums bill, previously thought to be an extreme measure, passed the House by voice vote in June 1985. The Senate rejected the bill, but the House action gave sanctions a new momentum.

The vote on the Dellums bill also drew attention to the increasing importance of black political power in the United States. Following passage of the Voting Rights Act of 1965, the number of registered black voters had risen markedly. In the South, black voter registration doubled in twenty years, growing from less than 2 million in 1968 to approximately 4 million in 1988. Many southern white members of Congress were elected with the help of the black vote and consequently became more responsive to civil rights issues and racial questions.

Blacks held key political offices in large American cities and counties, including New Orleans, Atlanta, Los Angeles, Detroit, Newark, Philadelphia, Washington, D.C., and Birmingham. According to the Joint Center for Political Studies, a private research organization, the number of black elected officials in the nation rose from 1,469 in 1970 to 6,056 in 1985, more than a fourfold increase in the fifteen-year period. By 1986 members of the Congressional Black Caucus chaired five of the twenty-two standing committees in the House of Representatives.

But the political dynamics of the anti-apartheid movement in the United States were not limited to black activism. The crisis in South Africa touched Americans of all colors and reached into corporate boardrooms, local legislatures, city councils, campuses, churches, and labor unions. The anti-apartheid campaign rekindled a collective spirit of social activism that had been dormant since the 1960s. Roman Catholic bishops, the major Protestant churches, and the National Council of Churches, to which most mainline Protestant and Orthodox churches belong, issued statements in favor of sanctions. Leaders of the country's largest civil rights organizations, labor unions, women's associations, and Jewish groups added their voices, including Coretta Scott King, Benjamin Hooks from the National Association for the Advancement of Colored People (NAACP), John Jacob from the National Urban League, Eleanor Smeal from the National Organization of Women, Henry Siegman from the American Jewish Congress, and the presidents of the largest AFL-CIO–affiliated unions.

Campus activism sharpened the debate. Shanties were erected as symbols of protest at colleges coast to coast. Students urged university trustees to sell their holdings in American companies doing business in South Africa. The objective for many, however, was not only to divest, that is, to end institutional investment in firms doing business in South Africa, but to force these corporations to disinvest, that is, to withdraw from South Africa completely.

The argument that the presence of U.S. corporations in South Africa would help blacks achieve their political rights lost much of its credibility during this period, especially after President Botha's so-called "Rubicon" speech on August 15, 1985. In this critical speech, Botha said that he had "crossed the Rubicon" in terms of his reform program, implying that he was committed to change, but at his own pace and on his own terms. Billed in advance by South African officials as conciliatory and as an occasion for announcing sweeping new reforms, the message instead was one of intransigence. Botha ruled out significant power sharing in South Africa and blamed the disturbances on "barbaric communist agitators . . . on the payroll of their masters far from this lovely country of ours." He declared: "I am not prepared to lead white South Africans and other minority groups on a road to abdication and suicide. Destroy white South Africa and our influence, and this country will drift into faction, chaos and poverty."

Botha's "Rubicon" speech marked a turning point in the U.S. debate. It "broke the backs of the university trustees" who were resisting pressure to take action against South Africa, and turned the tide of American public opinion, according to a researcher at the Investor Responsibility Research Center (IRRC), a Washington-based monitoring organization. University authorities were compelled to reassess a decade of resistance to divestment. One by one, major universities across the country, from the University of California on the west coast to Georgetown University in the east, divested.

Pressures on companies operating in South Africa increased significantly, not only from universities but also from local and state authorities, a number of which divested or passed antiprocurement legislation that prevented such corporations from bidding for public service contracts. California, for example, decided in August 1986 to require that nearly $11 billion of state investments in companies doing business in South Africa be withdrawn. In South Africa, a declining economy and a volatile political environment, in which the government rejected demands for change from its own business community, added to corporate frustrations. As a result of these pressures, there was a marked acceleration in the rate of U.S. corporations either pulling out of South Africa altogether or substantially reducing their involvement. More than half of the American firms with direct investments in South Africa withdrew between 1984 and the end of 1988.

Foreign bank loans to South Africa were also drying up. At the end of July 1985, Chase Manhattan Bank, followed by other American and European creditors, refused to roll over their short-term loans. The effect on South Africa was swift and painful. The value of the rand plunged and the government temporarily closed its currency and stock markets and froze repayment of its foreign debt. An international debt mediator had to be appointed, and protracted negotiations for rescheduling ensued between the government and South Africa's foreign creditors.

Commenting on these events, the *Financial Times* wrote: "The reality is the unexpected emergence of the banking system as a conduit for the U.S. public's attitude towards the situation in South Africa. It has allowed shareholders, depositors and the public directly to impose an economic sanction without having to persuade their government to do so."[27] A report by the U.S. General Accounting Office, the investigative arm of Congress, noted that researchers in both Europe and South Africa stated that Western banks' recall of loans has been the most effective economic pressure on South Africa.

U.S. activism was fed by increasing levels of South African government repression during this period. The government imposed a partial state of emergency on the areas of greatest unrest in July 1985, which was lifted eight months later. When the unrest continued, it declared a second state of emergency in June 1986, this time nationwide. The police and security forces were given virtually unlimited power to crush the uprising, now in its twenty-first month. Independent human rights groups estimated that in the period from September 1984 to mid-1986, twenty-five hundred people died, nearly all black, and at least thirty thousand were detained, including approximately three thousand children under eighteen.

Television had caught many of the details of the violence, from the "Trojan horse" tactics of the South African police, who opened fire on township residents without warning, to so-called black-on-black violence, in which mobs attacked people alleged to be collaborating with the government. After television cameras were banned from the townships in November 1985, these images were removed from American screens, drastically reducing the number of stories on South Africa broadcast by the American television networks. In August, for example, sixty-one stories were screened, but in the first month of the press restrictions, the number dropped to twenty.[28] Defending the government's actions, President Botha blamed the media for the violence, claiming that, wittingly or unwittingly, they were promoting turmoil by focusing on radical activists.

However, Pretoria's actions, designed to stall the sanctions momentum in the United States, were too late. Images of apartheid were off the television screens, but the issue remained high on legislative, academic, religious, corporate, and grassroots organizations' agendas. In fact, the anti-apartheid movement gained momentum during 1986. Apartheid was an issue with an appealing moral clarity, and sanctions and divestment offered tangible ways for Americans to express their feelings about officially sanctioned racism.

Eventually, even traditional opponents of sanctions began to shift ground. One notable example was the Reverend Leon H. Sullivan, a black Baptist minister from Philadelphia and a member of the board of General Motors. In 1977 Sullivan authored a voluntary code of conduct for American firms operating in South Africa known as the "Sullivan Principles" or "Sullivan Code." Initially, signatories to the code committed themselves to implementing a set of equal rights practices in the workplace and to funding social programs. The code was later expanded to include advocacy by the companies for fundamental political change.

The signatories argued that their presence in South Africa was a positive force for economic, social, and political change. In addition to implementing nondiscriminatory policies in the workplace and advocating the end of apartheid, they supported the process of black empowerment. They pointed out that over the course of a decade they had spent almost $250 million on education and training, community development, and social justice programs. Opponents of U.S. corporate investment in South Africa countered that the Sullivan Principles provided American companies with a rationale for staying in South Africa and their presence provided economic and political support for the South African government.

President Reagan's executive order on sanctions in September 1985 prescribed a code of conduct for U.S. corporations based on the Sullivan Principles, although no monitoring was required. This code was subsequently incorporated into the 1986 Comprehensive Anti-Apartheid Act as mandatory for firms with twenty-five employees or more.

Sullivan became increasingly disillusioned regarding the South African government's intentions, and he believed that the administration's policy had failed. He also apparently felt that the American business community had been insufficiently aggressive in pressing for political change in South Africa. In May 1985 Sullivan declared that if apartheid was not ended within two years, he would call for the withdrawal of American companies from South Africa and for an economic embargo of that country.

In June 1987 he made good his threat, calling not only for total U.S. disinvestment and an embargo, but also for breaking off diplomatic relations with South Africa. He praised the Sullivan signatory companies, saying that their efforts had "caused a revolution in industrial relations in South Africa." But he also stated that since it was "clear the South African government does not intend to end apartheid on its own . . . the strongest possible American non-violent protest" should be made.[29]

The Republicans' Dilemma. The debate over South Africa created an unexpected predicament for the White House and for the Republican Party. In an analysis of Republican Party reactions to apartheid during this period, William Finnegan wrote that "apartheid has divided the right more deeply than any other recent issue."[30] The issue became, simultaneously, an anti-Communist litmus test, a yardstick on racism, and a challenge to party loyalty. Whatever way it was cast, the controversy over South Africa drove a wedge between younger and older Republican party members that had a decisive effect on the ability of the administration to sustain political support for its policy.

The Conservative Opportunity Society (COS), a group of young House backbenchers led by Newt Gingrich (R–Georgia) and Vin Weber (R–Minnesota), saw the issue as potentially helpful in building a post-Reagan Republican consensus capable of making the party a majority organization. This meant encouraging blacks and young people to support the Republican Party, a strategy that required party members to distance themselves from the administration's South Africa policy.

The COS fired its first salvo against constructive engagement in December 1984, when thirty-five members of the group wrote a letter to South African Ambassador Bernardus G. Fourie warning that they would back sanctions unless Pretoria moved quickly to end apartheid. They noted that they were, for the most part, "politically conservative" and supported the administration's South African policy. However, they warned that "if constructive engagement becomes in your view an excuse for maintaining the unacceptable status quo, it will quickly become an approach that can engender no meaningful support among American policy-makers." Unless steps were taken to bring "an immediate end to the violence in South Africa accompanied by a demonstrated sense of urgency about ending apartheid," the ambassador was informed, the signatories would recommend that the U.S. government "curtail new American investment . . . and organize international diplomatic and economic sanctions against South Africa." (See Appendix B.) After sending the letter, Congressman Vin Weber commented: "We may not share the tactics of embassy demonstrators, but there is no ideological division in our minds in this country in our approach to apartheid."[31]

Support for UNITA was another area of conflict within the Republican Party. The COS, while moving toward punitive sanctions against South Africa, pushed for assistance to UNITA. The members of the COS saw no contradiction in this dual stand, since it was based on opposition to racism and communism. A small core of support for UNITA, which was heavily backed by South Africa, had existed for years among congressional conservatives. However, the "Reagan doctrine," which advocated modest amounts of aid for anti-Communist "freedom fighters" in the Third World, helped to broaden UNITA's appeal and give new impetus to the movement's cause on Capitol Hill. To clear the way for support for UNITA, the COS led the drive for the repeal of the Clark Amendment prohibiting U.S. aid for any of the factions in Angola's civil war. Ironically, the amendment was repealed on July 10, 1985, the same day the Senate voted overwhelmingly to impose economic sanctions against South Africa.

Crocker supported the repeal of the Clark Amendment but opposed providing aid to UNITA at that time, anticipating that it would set back his delicate negotiations on Namibia with the Angolan government. In deference to conservative sentiment, however, the White House overruled him. "We want Savimbi to know the cavalry is coming," said Reagan at a White House meeting when he signed the order authorizing the covert aid.[32] But Crocker's fears about Angola's reaction were vindicated. In retaliation, Angola broke off negotiations with the United States over the Namibian issue and the removal of Cuban troops in March 1986, creating a hiatus in official contacts that lasted until June 1987. Not until 1988, as the Reagan years were coming to a close, were serious negotiations resumed.

The Sanctions Struggle: 1985–86. Although Crocker still enjoyed the confidence of Secretary of State George Shultz, his control over southern Africa policy weakened as Congress, a White House staff concerned about Reagan's political image, and conservative ideologues in the administration began to assert their views.

Crocker had been sensitive to pressure from the right ever since his confrontation with Senator Helms during his protracted confirmation hearings. But as the voices of criticism from the right mounted, he neglected to take into account the possibility of a serious challenge from the left, with its strong drive for sanctions. The sanctions movement was beginning to receive support from moderates and conservatives in both parties, developments that took Crocker and the administration by surprise.

Although there were many nuanced views on the issue, the sanctions debate polarized basically into two camps. Crocker, along with other opponents of sanctions, argued that punitive measures would reduce U.S. leverage, make the South African government and the white population more intransigent, and encourage South African retaliation against its vulnerable black neighbors. Some of those opposing sanctions also suggested that South Africa might retaliate against the United States by cutting off supplies of strategic minerals, thereby forcing the United States to turn to the Soviet Union, the other major supplier. Opponents of U.S. sanctions also maintained that these measures would not work because South Africa could easily avoid them, especially since its other major trading partners—notably Britain and West Germany—were not prepared to take similar steps.

At the heart of their argument was the conviction, most consistently advanced by the administration, that economic progress under the capitalist system in South Africa would eventually make apartheid unworkable. It was also argued that sanctions would hurt blacks more than whites because blacks were more vulnerable. Moreover, opponents held that by weakening the South African business sector, which they believed was a progressive force that helped improve black living standards, sanctions would be counterproductive. Finally, opponents contended that more social and economic reforms had taken place under P. W. Botha than ever before in South Africa's history, and that sanctions would send the "wrong signal at the wrong time," making it politically impossible for Botha to continue his reform policy.

Sanctions supporters in Congress and elsewhere rejected these arguments, maintaining that the Reagan administration's tactic of quiet persuasion had not worked and that South Africa acted only under pressure. Sanctions would demonstrate that Washington was willing to exert pressure if Pretoria continued its policy of apartheid. Supporters acknowledged that sanctions by the United States would have limited effect if other trading partners of South Africa did not follow suit. They noted, however, that a similar lack of support had not stopped the United States from imposing sanctions against Libya, Nicaragua, Cuba, Poland, Iran, and the USSR in order to express strong political disapproval. They also argued that by setting an example, the United States could lead other countries to take similar actions.

The greatest threat to U.S. imports of South Africa's strategic minerals, the argument continued, came not from the risk of reprisals, but from a continuation of South Africa's apartheid policies, which eventually could lead to a level of internal disorder that would shut down the mines and disrupt production. The South African government would be highly unlikely to halt mineral exports to the West in retaliation for sanctions since this would cut off a major source of needed foreign exchange. The prospect of the United States becoming dependent on the Soviet Union was, in any case, exaggerated: Most U.S. needs could be met by alternative supplies, conservation, recycling, and substitution.

Sanctions supporters recognized that such measures might hurt blacks, but this concern was diluted by the frequent call for sanctions by credible black leaders in South Africa, including trade unionists, who said that blacks were hurt far more by apartheid. It was conceded that South Africa's economic system might be incompatible with apartheid and might even have some impact on its demise in the long term. This would take time, however. Moreover, the private sector had made no significant impact on the government's political strategy and had largely confined its actions to ending discrimination in the workplace. On the question of Botha's reforms, sanctions advocates pointed out that none of the steps taken by the South African government had addressed the central issue of political participation for blacks, the root cause of the turmoil in South Africa.

The prosanctions camp included a range of advocates, from those who supported comprehensive actions to those who advocated selective measures against South Africa, such as increasing the isolation of white South Africans by ending air links with the United States. Selective or targeted sanctions, it was argued, could send a strong signal to the South African government and the white community while minimizing the impact on blacks.

As the situation in South Africa deteriorated, and domestic pressure for U.S. action against Pretoria mounted, the role of Congress became critical. In 1985 the drive for sanctions was led by the Democratic-controlled House, where fifty-six Republicans, including a few conservatives, joined Democrats in a 295-to-127 vote favoring sanctions. Two conservative senators, William Roth, Jr., (R–Delaware) and Mitch McConnell (R–Kentucky), introduced a sanctions bill, raising doubts about the ability of the administration to hold the line in the Republican-controlled Senate as bipartisan dissatisfaction with the Reagan administration's policy increased. This made majority leader Robert Dole (R–Kansas), then a presidential hopeful, and Richard Lugar (R–Indiana), then chairman of the Senate Foreign

Relations Committee—both of whom were loyal Reagan supporters—pivotal actors during the 1985–86 debate.

A tough sanctions measure banning new loans, new investment,
computer sales, and imports of Krugerrands (South African gold
coins) had passed through the House in the summer of 1985. After
the disappointment of Botha's "Rubicon" speech and the failure of
the Reagan administration to produce any tangible results in its
diplomacy, a modified version of the bill was passed by the Senate,
and a House-Senate conference committee was scheduled to resolve
the differences.

In order to preempt legislatively imposed sanctions that would
be difficult to reverse, Dole and Lugar brokered a compromise with
the administration that resulted in an executive order by the president imposing limited sanctions in September 1985. The order was
based on the pending House bill. It banned Krugerrands, incorporated the Sullivan Principles into law, and restricted bank loans and
technology exports. However, it dropped a key provision that automatically would have triggered further sanctions a year later unless
South Africa adopted significant political reforms. It also left the
authority for lifting sanctions in the hands of the executive branch
rather than the Congress.

The president's executive order called for the creation of a
bipartisan advisory committee to examine U.S. policy toward South
Africa and make recommendations to the secretary of state. The
president's aim in setting up the committee was to forge a political
consensus that would head off another congressional attack. Meanwhile, the administration, with bipartisan congressional support,
more than doubled U.S. aid for black South Africans, from $8
million in FY 1985 to $19 million in FY 1986.

While it represented an attempt at compromise, the president's
executive order pleased neither the left nor the right. The left was
unhappy with Reagan's move because it was seen as a substitute for
more comprehensive sanctions. Calls for tougher measures continued from congressional Democrats. On the other hand, hard-line
conservatives believed Reagan's willingness to adopt limited sanctions would tilt the United States toward South African black radi-
cals and play into the hands of the Soviet Union.

The president insisted that the executive order was neither a
tactical maneuver nor a strategic retreat. When a reporter asked if
constructive engagement was still U.S. policy, Reagan replied: "Yes.
You might add the word 'active' to 'constructive.' But I think it still is
[the policy]. It is consistent with what we've been doing."[33] Notwithstanding the denial, it was clear that any form of sanctions was a

major setback for a policy that was built around persuasion, one that had explicitly and consistently ruled out punitive measures.

The fight over sanctions, wrote Finnegan, now had become not so much a contest between left and right as a struggle "for the soul of the Republican party." It pitted pragmatists against the rightwing in a bitter ideological debate during a midterm election year (1986) in which the Republicans were to lose control of the Senate. During the ensuing intraparty struggle, Howard Phillips, national director of the Conservative Caucus, a far-rightwing pressure group founded in 1974 that had gained some influence with the White House, "publicly threatened political reprisals against House Republicans who had 'joined the anti–South Africa lynch mob,'" Finnegan reported, "singling out Jack Kemp's 1988 presidential hopes for destruction if he did not change his vote in support of sanctions." Sensing the dissension among Republicans, Senator Edward Kennedy (D–Massachusetts), who had made a widely publicized and controversial visit to South Africa in January 1985, challenged Republicans to decide "whether they are the party of Lincoln or the party of apartheid."

The administration appeared to assume that popular opposition to constructive engagement resulted from its failure to convey the essence of the policy effectively, a shortcoming that could be rectified by explaining constructive engagement in a more systematic fashion. In September 1985, after the president's executive order, an ad hoc working group on South Africa, with a staff of over twenty people, was appointed at the State Department. Douglas Hollady, a White House aide, was given the rank of ambassador and put in charge. The group was not supposed to focus on the substance of policy, but rather on its presentation to the public.

However, the real cause of the public's growing disenchantment was the policy itself, particularly its inability to influence South Africa's behavior in the region or to move Pretoria to share political power with blacks. As the *Economist* had noted earlier, "The policy of constructive engagement required some emphatic success if it was not to be seen as a mere dodging of the apartheid issue."

A glimmer of hope about resolving the crisis in South Africa appeared in late 1985, with the formation of a Commonwealth peace initiative led by a seven-person international delegation known as the Eminent Persons Group (EPG). The mission, whose progress was watched closely by the international community, spent six months attempting to facilitate a dialogue between the South African government and anti-apartheid leaders. On May 19, 1986, as the EPG appeared to be on the verge of reaching agreement on "a negotiating concept," Pretoria launched a three-pronged ground and air attack against alleged ANC bases in Zimbabwe, Botswana, and Zambia—all Commonwealth members—and rationalized the action by comparing it to the U.S. antiterrorist bombings in Libya a month earlier.

Although South Africa had been destabilizing its neighbors for some time, these raids provoked a particularly strong international reaction because they occurred while a peace initiative was under way. Moreover, they had no military purpose. Zambia, the political and administrative headquarters of the ANC, is a thousand miles from Pretoria; Zimbabwe had refused to permit the ANC to use its territory for guerrilla activities; and Botswana had expelled its few ANC political representatives months before under pressure from Pretoria. The raiders did not hit key military installations or command centers. Furthermore, the comparison with Libya was infuriating to the Reagan administration. In response, the United States recalled its military attaché from Pretoria and expelled his South African counterpart. Secretary Shultz stated that Pretoria's action was "totally without justification and is completely unacceptable," the toughest language the Reagan administration had used to criticize Pretoria's regional activities.

The major casualty of the attacks was the Commonwealth peace initiative. In June 1986 the EPG issued its report, concluding that the South African government had demonstrated no genuine intention to dismantle apartheid or to enter into negotiations with bona fide black leaders. Commonwealth leaders met in August and, with the exception of Britain, agreed to impose limited economic sanctions against South Africa.

The Commonwealth action intensified the call for stiffer sanctions in the United States, this time with moderate Republicans leading the way. As the next round of the sanctions debate began in the summer of 1986, Senators Lugar and Dole joined Nancy Kassebaum (R–Kansas), the chairperson of the Senate Subcommittee on African Affairs, to warn Reagan that unless he moved forcefully to pressure the Pretoria government, Congress would legislate further sanctions.

The president's earlier executive order, which was meant to hold the line against sanctions, had in reality intensified the debate. The question was no longer whether sanctions would be imposed, but rather which sanctions would be the most effective. The three key Senate Republicans—Dole, Lugar, and Kassebaum—repeatedly appealed to the White House to avoid a congressional showdown and accept a compromise package of stiffer measures.

The administration began negotiating with Senate leaders, but in the end the president flatly rejected their advice. His decision was strongly influenced by Patrick Buchanan, an aggressive rightwing syndicated columnist and former speechwriter for President Nixon, who was a firm supporter of the South African government. As Reagan's communications director, Buchanan had a unique platform from which to shape the president's responses. Perhaps his moment of greatest influence came when he drafted the critical speech on South Africa that President Reagan delivered on television on July 22, 1986.[34] (See Appendix C.)

"The Speech That Launched a Thousand Critics" was the headline in the *New York Times* the next day. "Perhaps no other speech in the Reagan presidency has stirred as much internal opposition and bipartisan criticism as President Reagan's address . . . on South African policy, according to White House aides," reported the paper.

Reagan stood firm in his belief that Pretoria deserved to be defended and he praised Pretoria's "dramatic change." "Indeed, it is because State President Botha has presided over . . . reforms," Reagan declared, "that [white] extremists have denounced him as a traitor." The ANC, South Africa's oldest and most popular liberation movement, which is banned in South Africa, and other antiapartheid groups were referred to as radical organizations engaged in acts of "calculated terror" in order to bring on racial war through "Soviet-armed guerrillas." Using Buchanan's inflammatory language, which mirrored Pretoria's, the president declared that "the South African government is under no obligation to negotiate the future of the country with any organization that proclaims a goal of creating a Communist state and uses terrorist tactics and violence to achieve it."

There was considerable confusion within the administration at this juncture. On the day after Reagan's speech, which flatly opposed sanctions, Shultz told the Senate Foreign Relations Committee that the administration might join its European allies in imposing additional curbs against South Africa if Pretoria did not initiate negotiations to end apartheid. However, it was Reagan's words, not Shultz's attempts to soften congressional criticism, that framed the policy debate. The president's unyielding stance triggered a strong political reaction, much in the same way that Botha's "Rubicon" address had done the previous year.

The impact of the speech was summed up by Simon Barber, a Washington-based British journalist specializing in U.S.–South African relations. "The text [of the speech], while critical of the South African government, simply did not address domestic or South African political reality," he wrote. "Indeed, it seemed deliberately calculated to provoke the worst possible responses from all sides: it gave Pretoria comfort, black South Africa reason to despair, and Congress no choice."[35]

Political and moral concerns became paramount, convincing many skeptics that sanctions would have to be used. Senator Kassebaum summed up this sentiment at the peak of the debate on the Senate floor: "Whatever the shortcomings [of sanctions legislation] . . . they are far less onerous than a failure to respond to the challenge of the present moment." The objectives, she said, were "to correct the South African misperception that [Pretoria] has tacit Western approval for its course of gradualist reform without political change, . . . to show white South Africans that intransigence will have tangible costs for them, . . . and to preserve our role as an honest broker in the South African dilemma."[36]

The outcome was an open break with the president by Republican senators just three months before the critical midterm election in November 1986. Disappointed by Reagan's speech, Dole, Lugar, Kassebaum, and several other Senate Republicans joined members of the COS, liberal Democrats like Howard Wolpe (D–Michigan) and Stephen Solarz, and members of the Congressional Black Caucus in support of tougher sanctions. The main objective of the Republican leadership was to limit the political damage that had been created by an unpopular and ineptly managed policy. Congress recognized what the White House refused to acknowledge: The debate had become a domestic political issue. The vote on South Africa was portrayed not only as a key foreign policy decision but as a test of where Congress stood on racism. "Let's face it," said Bob Dole, "there's a lot of politics involved. . . . this has now become a domestic civil rights issue."[37]

The Comprehensive Anti-Apartheid Act of 1986. In August the Comprehensive Anti-Apartheid Act (CAAA) was passed easily by both houses of Congress and vetoed by the president. (See Appendix D.) On October 3, 1986, the veto was overturned by an overwhelming majority in both the Senate and the House of Representatives. It was one of the most decisive defeats for Reagan's foreign policy during his eight years in the White House, astonishing many political observers at home and abroad.

The legislation imposed the strongest set of sanctions yet taken against Pretoria by one of its major Western trading partners, even though it did not call for a total embargo or compulsory disinvestment. Its main provisions banned new investments and bank loans, which had virtually dried up anyway; ended South African air links with the U.S.; and prohibited a range of South African imports, including coal, uranium, steel, textiles, and agricultural products. The legislation also threatened to cut off military aid to allies suspected of breaching the international arms embargo against Pretoria, a provision that had serious implications for Israel since that country had become an important source of arms and military expertise for South Africa. Finally, the president was required to deliver a report to Congress on an annual basis detailing progress in South Africa toward ending apartheid and recommending additional punitive measures if there was no substantial progress.

But there was more to the act than sanctions. Running to over thirty pages, the purpose of the legislation, as its name implies, was to "set forth a comprehensive and complete framework to guide the efforts of the United States in helping to bring an end to apartheid in South Africa and lead to the establishment of a nonracial, democratic form of government."

In short, the law was intended to establish a new U.S. policy to replace constructive engagement. Guidance was given on the policies the United States should adopt toward Pretoria, the black-controlled states in the region, and the ANC; the role of the Western allies on sanctions; the elements of a negotiated political solution in South Africa; and the U.S. position on matters ranging from aid for black South African education and labor unions to the U.S. attitude toward "necklacing." It also spelled out measures the South African government could take to have sanctions lifted. These included an internationally recognized Namibian settlement, the release of political prisoners, an end to the state of emergency, and lifting the bans on proscribed anti-apartheid organizations.

The act also had a strong anti-Communist flavor. While it criticized Pretoria on apartheid, it also questioned the beliefs and tactics of the ANC and the Pan-Africanist Congress (PAC), another exiled black South African nationalist movement with a much smaller following. It revealed a special congressional concern with the South African Communist Party (SACP), a close ally of the ANC. In the act, Congress required the administration to prepare eleven reports in addition to the annual assessments of overall progress. They included one on the degree to which "Communists have infiltrated the many black and nonwhite South African organizations engaged in the fight against the apartheid system."

The broad and sometimes contradictory provisions of the legislation led to some confusion about its real purpose. For some, the legislation was not intended to be punitive but was seen as the only way of sending a strong message to the South African government that it should change its policies. For others, the sanctions in the act were taken seriously as a means of punishing Pretoria. For a third group, domestic considerations were predominant. Many members of Congress felt the need to respond to the sentiments of their constituents, and others saw an opportunity to inflict a foreign policy defeat on the Reagan administration. Special interests also played a part in shaping the legislation. Strategic minerals, for example, were excluded from the list of banned South African imports. Protectionist lobbies affiliated with coal, textiles, and agricultural products benefited from sanctions. But while these private interest groups may have had their own reasons for jumping on the anti-apartheid bandwagon, they did not play a prominent role in devising the legislation or pushing it through.

Essentially, whatever the personal motivation of individual members, Congress abandoned the president because his policy had lost credibility at home. After six years, it had made only marginal progress on its regional objectives and, more important, it had failed to respond to the crisis inside South Africa. While congressional Democrats exhibited considerable passion, moderate Republicans had to do some soul-searching. Some Republican senators expressed regret that the administration's mishandling of the issue, particularly its tendency to antagonize critics it might otherwise have won over, had forced Congress to enact sanctions. "We should have never reached this point on the sanctions issue if we had had strong and focused leadership," commented Senator Kassebaum, an original supporter of constructive engagement who had become disillusioned with the way the policy had been implemented and with its lack of results. She voted against the president more in sorrow than in anger, knowing that the mutiny within the party would hurt his image as a leader.[38]

The CAAA was a watershed in U.S.–South African relations because it established for the first time that the South African government would have to pay a price for the suppression of black protest and for withholding blacks' political rights. The legislation demolished a traditional U.S. policy premise holding that the threat of sanctions against South Africa was more effective than sanctions themselves. In passing the CAAA, Congress concluded that threatening South Africa was no longer sufficient and that a credible policy had to be based on tangible pressure. Moreover, this new U.S.–South African relationship was institutionalized in law and could be changed only with the consent of the Congress.

After Sanctions

South Africa's salience as a U.S. foreign policy issue diminished during the last two years of the Reagan presidency. The impact of other foreign policy questions and the American public's relatively short attention span for specific foreign affairs topics were partly responsible. But the most important reason was the success of the South African government in crushing internal dissent and muzzling local and foreign media. After 1985 Americans saw virtually nothing on their television screens and read little in their newspapers about the South African crisis and the continuing though diminished unrest.

The final Reagan years, however, were not uneventful. The administration, Congress, state and city governments, U.S. corporations, and countless grassroots organizations continued to play important advocacy and public education roles. Following the passage of the CAAA, an incisive critique of constructive engagement was published by a prestigious bipartisan panel; the administration made tactical shifts that helped blunt criticism of its policy; there was a determined though largely unsuccessful conservative offensive in Congress and elsewhere against Angola, Mozambique, and the other member-states of the Southern African Development Coordination Conference (SADCC); and liberal activism continued. Finally, in the closing days of the administration, critical changes in U.S.-Soviet relations and in the balance of power in southern Africa enabled Chester Crocker to resume his regional diplomacy and bring it to a successful conclusion.

The Shultz Advisory Committee Report. In January 1987, during a lull between the debate over sanctions and a renewed drive by conservatives to help insurgents in Angola and Mozambique, the report by the Secretary of State's Advisory Committee on South Africa, created by Reagan in September 1985, was published. Entitled *A U.S. Policy Toward South Africa*, the report was released after the public debate had peaked and sanctions legislation had been enacted. It therefore failed to generate much media attention, to influence Congress, or to alter the administration's policy. Moreover, there was some dissension among the committee's twelve members, who had been selected by Secretary Shultz. Three departed from the majority that supported sanctions, and two felt that a total U.S. trade embargo should be considered. Nonetheless, a remarkable degree of consensus existed within this bipartisan, blue-ribbon panel. Its report cogently summarized the state of U.S. policy and set out some guidelines for the future.

The policy of constructive engagement, the committee concluded, had "failed to achieve its objectives," and a new policy was required. The report recommended that the first priority of U.S. policy should be to help facilitate "good faith" negotiations between Pretoria and "representative leaders of the black majority aimed at shaping a nonracial democratic political system," and that the president himself should take the lead.

It urged the United States to clarify its opposition to apartheid, distance itself from South Africa's white-led reforms, provide more aid to the country's disadvantaged blacks, strengthen U.S. officials' ties to black leaders across the political spectrum, give greater assistance to the other states in the region, and internationalize existing U.S. sanctions. It also advised the administration to consider applying additional pressures unless the South African government lifted the state of emergency, released all political prisoners, and ended its ban on the ANC and other political parties. Many of these recommendations were a reaffirmation or an extension of the 1986 sanctions legislation.

The report also focused on some broader problems, notably the central inconsistency of the administration's policy:

> Any strategy for dealing with South Africa must be part of a broader regional strategy. Events in South Africa inevitably affect—and are in turn affected by—events elsewhere in southern Africa. Moreover, policy actions of the United States toward other nations of the region (for example, the 1986 decision to provide military assistance to Jonas Savimbi's . . . UNITA in Angola, to suspend aid to Zimbabwe, and to curtail pledged aid to Mozambique) inevitably affect US credibility with South Africans.

The committee accordingly asked the president "to take note" of the complications for U.S. policy in South Africa created by American military assistance to UNITA in Angola. On the threat of communism, the committee stated:

> We do not believe that the escalating conflict in South Africa will precipitate a major confrontation with the Soviet Union. While Moscow is certain to continue its policy of limited financial and military support for the African National Congress (ANC), and especially the South African Communist Party (SACP) component within the ANC, it shows no inclination to become directly involved. The Soviets do stand to gain considerably, however, if a protracted conflict in South Africa embitters that country's black majority against the West.

The Administration's Shift in Tactics. The main concern of the administration in the post-CAAA period was to avoid a recurrence of public controversy. Republican Party strategists and President Reagan's White House advisers saw apartheid as a "no-win" situation, a perception heightened by the approach of the 1988 presidential election campaign.

The Reagan administration's immediate response was to deny that the new law signaled a change in policy. It chose to treat sanctions not as a reversal but as an unwanted addition to its policy. While promising to implement the legislation, the administration vowed it would oppose further sanctions, vote against similar measures at the United Nations, and continue to press for change in South Africa through quiet diplomacy. Three months after sanctions were enacted, Secretary Shultz asserted that the fundamental elements of the policy were still intact:

> You don't just throw up your hands and say "I don't like it. I'm leaving." You stay there. You are, if I may use the term, engaged. So this is our policy—to be engaged, and engaged with everybody, and we hope that our actions will be constructive.[39]

Notwithstanding such pronouncements, the term "constructive engagement" disappeared from official statements. (The joke in some State Department circles was that it had become "the policy that dare not speak its name.")

In fact, at the height of the sanctions debate the previous summer, it had become apparent that the administration was already making tactical adjustments when it decided to replace Ambassador Herman Nickel, who was due to return home, with a black ambassador. The State Department characterized this move as part of the normal rotation of ambassadors, but the decision was widely interpreted by observers in Washington as a tactic to deflect some of the criticism of constructive engagement and to remove the perception that the United States was closely aligned with South Africa's whites and their government.

Robert J. Brown, a black businessman from North Carolina, was announced as the leading candidate for the post by the White House in July 1986. Brown's candidacy soon ran into trouble when it was revealed that he had ties with a former Nigerian politician who had been accused of corruption. Brown withdrew. A second suggested candidate was Terence A. Todman, a career diplomat who was then serving as ambassador to Denmark. Todman effectively disqualified himself at a press conference he called in Copenhagen where he stated that, while the job had not been formally offered to him, he could not consider it because U.S. policy toward South Africa lacked credibility.

The third person canvassed for the job was Edward J. Perkins, another career foreign service officer, who was ambassador to Liberia at the time. He was nominated and quickly approved by the Senate two weeks after the CAAA became law. In the end, the State Department found a suitable envoy, but the lengthy and highly publicized search caused the administration considerable embarrassment.

Another indication of a tactical shift by the administration was the meeting between Secretary Shultz and Oliver Tambo, the president of the ANC, in January 1987. Only seven months earlier, State Department officials in Washington had refused to meet Alfred Nzo, the ANC general secretary, while he was visiting the United States. Regular and high-level official contacts with ANC leaders had been discouraged, largely for fear of upsetting the South African government. However, Tambo had met Crocker in London in September 1986, and other lower-level contacts had taken place between the ANC and State Department officials at various times.

In addition to the Shultz meeting, which was the ANC's first encounter with U.S. officials at the cabinet level in the organization's seventy-five year history, the administration changed its public characterization of the ANC. Instead of casting it as a Communist-backed organization that uses "calculated terror," as Reagan described it in his July 1986 speech, the State Department now described the group as having "a legitimate voice" in South Africa.

The Shultz-Tambo meeting was a significant diplomatic victory for the ANC that angered the rightwing in the United States—a number of people demonstrated outside the State Department during the talks—and annoyed Pretoria. However, higher-level meetings had occurred between the administration and other black leaders from southern Africa. President Reagan had met previously with Archbishop Desmond Tutu; Chief Mangosuthu Gatsha Buthelezi, the Zulu homeland leader; and Jonas Savimbi, the Angolan guerrilla leader. Also, the Shultz-Tambo meeting revealed substantial disagreements. Shultz told Tambo that he had grave reservations about the ANC because of its endorsement of violence and its links with the South African Communist Party, two issues that the South African government consistently raised. Nevertheless, this greater recognition of an organization that had widespread support among blacks in South Africa and the region reflected a broadening of U.S. policy and a search for new directions.

The administration also began to spell out its ideas on the political future of South Africa in more specific terms than it had in the past. Secretary Shultz, in a speech entitled "The Democratic Future of South Africa," delivered on September 29, 1987, said that he wanted South Africans to know what the United States was for as well as what it was against. South Africa should have "a democratic electoral system with multiparty participation and universal franchise for all adult South Africans," constitutional guarantees for human rights, an independent judiciary, and an economic system that "guarantees economic freedom for every South African."

In South Africa, Ambassador Perkins kept a low profile in his first year, but gradually assumed a more visible position, particularly in the black community and with anti-apartheid leaders. He also elaborated on both the nature and the manner of achieving a desirable political solution to South Africa's problems. In an outspoken article in the December 1987 issue of *Leadership,* an influential South African magazine, Perkins described apartheid as "one of the century's most disastrous feats of social engineering." Perkins's article, in which he also argued that more pressure should be applied to South Africa, drew fire from Pretoria. "How the present or any future South African government sees its future is none of his business," the South African Foreign Ministry retorted.[40] But Perkins continued to speak out, thereby stretching the administration's definition of quiet diplomacy.

Improved relations with the black states of southern Africa were another measure of the administration's tactical realignment. Previously, the Reagan administration had shown little enthusiasm for SADCC, the principal regional economic organization. Comprising nine black-ruled states, SADCC had been founded in 1980 with the twin goals of reducing its members' economic dependence on

South Africa and fostering regional development. For the first six years of SADCC's existence, the United States had granted it only small amounts of aid, preferring to funnel assistance to individual SADCC countries on a bilateral basis. In addition, the administration had voiced skepticism about the pace and efficiency of SADCC's development strategy and its capacity to reduce the region's dependence on South Africa.

However, in late 1986 the administration appeared to change its mind. It proposed a new multiyear Initiative for Economic Progress in Southern Africa just at the time that Congress was moving to bar funds to countries in the region. Then, at the eighth annual meeting of SADCC nations and donors in Gaborone, Botswana, in February 1987, the USAID administrator, Peter McPherson, announced that the United States would commit $93 million over an eighteen-month period as a vote of confidence in the economic future of southern Africa. This was the first time that a top U.S. official had attended a SADCC meeting. In a speech in June 1987 assessing U.S. relations with the region, Michael Armacost, under secretary of state for political affairs, noted that "many Southern African governments are turning away from collectivist practices to the free market. We want to encourage this by providing help in making this welcome transition." Since 1987 the United States has provided $50 million annually to SADCC in addition to bilateral aid to individual member-states.

At the same time, the Reagan administration's relations with Pretoria had cooled, mainly as a result of South Africa's destabilization strategy. This was symbolized in June 1985 when Ambassador Nickel was recalled for three months following repeated attacks by South Africa against its neighbors. Relations were also strained because of South Africa's harsh repression of black protest and the passage of the CAAA. On the one hand, Pretoria lost confidence in President Reagan's ability to control his own policy; on the other, the administration, responding to domestic dissatisfaction, became more openly critical of the South African government's actions. By the end of 1987, the *Citizen,* a progovernment South African newspaper, commented: "Looking back over the past year, it is clear that the United States has become South Africa's enemy number one (leaving aside Russia and Communist-bloc countries . . .)."

On the question of sanctions, however, little changed in Washington. A few people in the administration, such as Ambassador Perkins, believed that sanctions had been successful in sending a signal of U.S. support to South Africa's blacks and argued that a good case existed for applying further selective sanctions against

South Africa. The official line was clear, however. In February 1987 the administration vetoed a UN Security Council resolution calling for nearly identical sanctions to those mandated by the CAAA, placing the United States in the anomalous position of voting against the spirit of its own law in an international forum.

The Conservatives' Offensive. The debate over South Africa had temporarily obscured the activities of a number of conservative groups concerned with southern Africa. Strong supporters of the Reagan Doctrine, these groups focused their attention on supporting "pro-Western freedom fighters" and undermining "Soviet-backed Marxist" governments. Their principal targets were Angola and Mozambique. They also were fiercely hostile to the ANC and its ally, the South African Communist Party. This conservative agenda was supported by several organizations, including the Heritage Foundation and the Conservative Caucus. It also had considerable backing in the White House, and was strongly endorsed by the *Washington Times,* a daily newspaper owned by the Unification Church that began publishing in 1982 and produced regular if often partisan coverage of southern Africa.

On some issues, such as U.S. aid for UNITA in Angola and sanctions against South Africa, these groups agreed with U.S. policy. On other issues, like the administration's support for the FRELIMO government in Mozambique and its new high-level dialogue with the ANC, they were diametrically opposed. President Reagan's own ambivalent views about U.S. policy toward southern Africa were sometimes a source of comfort, and at other times a matter of concern to conservatives. Early in his administration, the president had jokingly admitted that there was some confusion about where he stood in relation to his conservative supporters. "Sometimes our right hand doesn't know what our far-right hand is doing," he said.[41]

The conservatives first turned their attention to Angola. UNITA had many supporters among the American right, and had hired a Washington public relations firm that ran a highly successful campaign promoting the movement's cause. Jonas Savimbi, UNITA's leader, was a particular favorite of William Casey, the director of the Central Intelligence Agency (CIA), who visited him at his headquarters in Jamba, Angola, in 1985, the year the Clark Amendment was repealed. Casey regarded the lifting of restrictions on U.S. aid to UNITA as a personal victory.[42] In June of that year, Citizens for America, a conservative lobbying group led by Lewis E. Lehrman, a millionaire Republican, organized a conference of guerrilla leaders who were fighting Soviet-supported governments in Africa, Asia, and Central America. The meeting took place in Jamba and Lehrman delivered a letter to Savimbi from President Reagan expressing moral support for UNITA.[43]

The conservatives targeted the U.S. oil companies—of which Chevron was the most important—that had long played a dominant role in the production of Angola's oil, the source of most of the country's foreign exchange. In November 1986 they persuaded Congress to no longer allow American companies operating in Angola to deduct taxes paid to Angola from their U.S. taxes.[44]

The conservatives' considerable strength and reach extended to key congressional players. At the behest of the Conservative Caucus, for example, Senator Helms sent out letters in April 1987 to 30,000 of Chevron's 220,000 shareholders to protest the company's Angolan holdings on the ground that they were generating hard currency to help pay for Soviet military equipment and Cuban troops. Cuban forces in Angola helped protect American commercial interests by guarding Chevron's facilities against guerrilla attacks from UNITA. Chevron argued that it took no political position in Angola and that its presence there was purely a commercial operation under a contract that predated Angolan independence. Nevertheless, the congressional offensive continued, and a move in 1987 to prohibit the Department of Defense from buying Angolan raw materials, such as oil, only narrowly failed.

Following the administration's decision in 1986 to supply arms to UNITA, several conservative organizations formed a pressure group known as the Coalition to Restore A More Benevolent Order (RAMBO). RAMBO wanted the United States to end its economic ties with Angola. It received support from some individuals who were not usually thought of as conservatives. For example, Congressman Claude Pepper (D–Florida), while liberal on many issues, was probably influenced by the presence of a large number of anti-Castro Cuban-Americans in his district.

Another Democrat with a diverse voting record who also supported UNITA was Senator Dennis DeConcini of Arizona. His interest derived from parallels he saw between events in Angola, Afghanistan, and Nicaragua. In these countries, the Soviet Union had significantly increased its influence, with little opposition from the United States. DeConcini supported sanctions against South Africa but believed in a tough line against what he saw as Soviet and Cuban aggression in Angola.[45] Accordingly, he backed legislation introduced in the House of Representatives in December 1986 by Pepper, Dante Fascell (D–Florida), and Jack Kemp (R–New York) that called for a total trade embargo against Angola, seeing it as a way to press for a settlement in the country's civil war and force withdrawal of Cuban troops. While this move failed, a less sweeping measure, sponsored by Senator Bob Graham (D–Florida), which suspended the most-favored-nation status for Angola for a period of six months, was passed as part of a trade bill in 1987.

In June 1988 DeConcini formed the Angola Task Force, a bipartisan, pro-Savimbi group of fifteen senators that pressed for a power-sharing role for UNITA in the Angolan government.[46] Support for Savimbi was not limited to the members of the Angola Task Force. In May 1988 thirty senators, ranging across the political spectrum from liberal Christopher Dodd (D–Connecticut) to conservative Jesse Helms (R–North Carolina), signed a letter to President Reagan urging him to press the Soviets to help achieve an end to the Angolan civil war and the formation of a government of national reconciliation at his fourth summit with General Secretary Mikhail Gorbachev in Moscow. A similar letter signed by forty-five members of the House of Representatives was also sent.

In principle, the administration opposed congressional measures to restrict U.S. trade with Angola because they infringed on the freedom of the executive branch to conduct foreign policy. Nonetheless, it was sympathetic to the Angola Task Force's attempts to support UNITA. In June 1987 a second grant of $15 million in covert military aid, which included Stinger antiaircraft and TOW antitank missiles, was approved. The administration justified its decision by saying that the Soviet Union had supplied the Angolan government with over $1 billion worth of military aid in the past year to support a major offensive against UNITA.

The decision to continue military aid to UNITA was consistent with the Reagan doctrine and pleased conservatives. However, it highlighted the administration's growing policy contradictions, not only in the region, where it supported black "Marxist" governments in such countries as Mozambique and Zimbabwe and opposed the so-called pro-Western dissident movements fighting those governments, but also with regard to Angola itself. Just as the new aid package to UNITA was being announced, for example, the State Department was preparing to receive a delegation of senior Angolan officials; this was the first such meeting since the Angolan government had broken off negotiations in March 1986 in response to the U.S. decision to arm UNITA.

The conservatives also focused on U.S. support for SADCC. They were hostile to SADCC because most of its member states supported sanctions against South Africa and were sympathetic to the ANC. In one of its most provocative measures, Congress adopted an amendment introduced by Senator Larry Pressler (R–South Dakota) to the supplemental appropriations bill. Enacted in July 1987, the amendment prohibited aid "for activities in Mozambique and Angola," barred funds for some of the most vital rail and road links in southern Africa, and made some $40 million of U.S. economic assistance to SADCC members, which was authorized in the legislation, conditional on certification by the administration that recipient countries were not protecting individuals or groups that participated in or condoned "necklacing." It did not affect foreign aid funds authorized in other legislation.

The proposal won the support of some liberals, such as Senators Tom Harkin (D–Iowa) and Barbara Mikulski (D–Maryland), because they did not want to go on record as opposing a "human rights amendment." Cast as an antiterrorism measure, the Pressler amendment was really an attempt to penalize the SADCC states for supporting the ANC and sanctions against South Africa.

The amendment provoked a storm of protest among the black states in the region. In a *Foreign Affairs* article, President Mugabe of Zimbabwe wrote:

> No country in the region has ever condoned the practice [of necklacing] nor has any South African liberation movement. We have condemned it forthrightly from every public platform. . . . We in the region regard that vote in Congress as an attempt to blackmail us into supporting apartheid, since it concerns a practice over which we have no control whatsoever. . . .[47]

In fact, the administration certified that none of the SADCC states approved of "necklacing." "The result," commented one administration official, "was that no one lost a penny."[48]

The conservatives' heaviest and most sustained attack, however, was directed against their third target, Mozambique. Their view was that the Reagan doctrine should apply to RENAMO's insurgency against the FRELIMO government just as it did to UNITA's rebellion against the MPLA government in Angola. Both rebel groups were, in the conservatives' eyes, made up of legitimate anti-Communist "freedom fighters" who deserved U.S. support.

In effect, opposition to Mozambique became a rallying point for the right, just as sanctions against South Africa had been for the left. Rightwing groups, such as the Heritage Foundation, Free the Eagle, and the Conservative Action Foundation—rival organizations that accused each other of having been infiltrated by Communist agents and of falsely representing RENAMO—opposed the Nkomati Accord in March 1984 and President Samora Machel's visit to the White House later that year. Although Mozambique, under Machel's successor, Joaquim Chissano, continued to move closer to the West, this did not change the views of the anti-Mozambican groups in the United States.

Senator Helms first singled out Mozambique in FY 1985, when he succeeded in amending the appropriations bill to prohibit a modest military training program for Mozambique. The amendment was renewed each year. In 1987 he broadened his attack, targeting the administration's nominee for ambassador to Mozambique. With the support of twenty-eight senators, he used the delaying tactics he had employed so effectively against Crocker in 1981 to hold up the nomination of Melissa Wells, an experienced and highly regarded career foreign service officer. After eleven months of hearings and procedural delays, he lifted his objection and she was finally confirmed in September 1987.

The conservatives' position on RENAMO, though strongly opposed by the State Department, elicited sympathy in parts of the bureaucracy and in the White House. When Edward J. Feulner, president of the Heritage Foundation, was appointed a political consultant to the White House in March 1987, he promoted RENAMO, whose representatives operated out of the foundation's offices in Washington. At various times, officials responsible for Africa in the National Security Council, the CIA, and the Defense Intelligence Agency were disposed to help RENAMO, which also received strong support from the *Washington Times*.

Crocker, however, with the backing of Shultz, drew a sharp distinction between RENAMO and UNITA. He argued that UNITA had a long history of resistance; a popular base among the Ovimbundu, the largest ethnic group in Angola, which accounted for roughly 40 percent of the population; and a coherent and well-established leadership. RENAMO, Crocker pointed out, shared none of these characteristics.

In one of his strongest statements supporting the Mozambican government, Crocker confronted the rightwing directly, telling the Senate Subcommittee on African Affairs in June 1987 that the United States had no legitimate grounds for initiating an official relationship with RENAMO, a position that, ironically, drew praise from TransAfrica's Randall Robinson, Crocker's nemesis on South Africa. Following a massacre of nearly four hundred civilians in Mozambique that was attributed to RENAMO, Robinson defended the beleaguered assistant secretary in an article in the *Washington Post* in August 1987: "For once," Robinson wrote, "the Reagan Administration is on the sensible side in southern Africa, supporting the Mozambican government."

A study on RENAMO's conduct of the insurgency in Mozambique was released in April 1988. The report, commissioned by the State Department and written by Robert Gersony, an independent expert on refugees, focused on the plight of Mozambique's uprooted population. Its most condemnatory passages concerned refugee accounts of the atrocities committed by RENAMO. According to the report, RENAMO had been responsible for the murder of an estimated one hundred thousand civilians and had caused well over two hundred thousand Mozambicans to become refugees. The report said that RENAMO "uses captive labor, rape, mutilation and even arbitrary execution as tactics in its struggle to overthrow the government." The Gersony Report had a significant political impact. By discrediting the guerrillas, it undermined the case of their American backers and vindicated the administration's support for the FRELIMO government.

Nevertheless, the dispute over RENAMO continued throughout the remainder of the Reagan presidency, with the conservatives harassing but not seriously damaging the administration's friendly relations with Mozambique. In FY 1987 Congress proscribed the use of foreign aid funds for Mozambique unless the president certified that it was in the national interest. Reagan made the certification in FY 1987 and FY 1988 before the requirement was dropped in FY 1989. U.S. aid to Mozambique soared in this period. Mozambique received more than $200 million in U.S. assistance in the form of regional funds, bilateral economic aid, food aid, disaster assistance, and SADCC railroad funds. Nearly half of it was delivered when the conservatives' offensive was at its peak in 1987–88, a measure of the administration's success in defending its policy. In fact, by the end of the Reagan administration, Mozambique had become the largest recipient of U.S. aid in sub-Saharan Africa.

The Liberals: A Continuing Activism. While conservatives focused their attention on the black-ruled states of southern Africa and the administration's contacts with the ANC, liberals pressed for further economic penalties against the South African government. However, like the administration, they changed their tactics. Pressure in Congress for additional sanctions continued, but liberal activism returned to the state and local levels and to the issues of divestment and disinvestment.

The anti-apartheid movement was constrained at this time by several factors. Pretoria's crackdown on dissent and the drastic reduction in news from South Africa made it more difficult to sustain interest in South Africa and pressure against constructive engagement. At the same time, the waning of public interest in South Africa helped the administration maintain a low profile on the issue. Moreover, the administration's own tactical shifts achieved a measure of success in dampening criticism. Its high-level contacts with the ANC, its new policy of backing the SADCC countries with significant amounts of aid, and the deterioration of its relations with Pretoria all enabled it to argue that it had broadened its contacts and shifted ground in southern Africa. Finally, the revival of Crocker's regional diplomacy, especially when it began to show signs of producing results, caused many of the administration's liberal opponents to exercise restraint since they shared Crocker's goals if not his tactics.

Ironically, the anti-apartheid movement's success in driving sanctions through Congress, over Reagan's veto, also slowed its momentum. Congressional sanctions had two aims: to send a strong message to South Africa and to condemn the administration's policy. Once those goals were achieved, it became clear that liberal activists had not developed a strategy for the next move except to press for more sanctions. Furthermore, many sanctions supporters closer to the center of the political spectrum argued for a moratorium on new legislation in order to assess the effectiveness of the CAAA. The result was less concentration on Congress and sanctions and more attention to grassroots efforts against American corporations still operating in South Africa and the institutions holding stock in those companies.

The rate of corporate withdrawal from South Africa began to ebb after reaching a peak in the mid-1980s. In 1987 fifty-six companies withdrew; the following year the number dropped to twenty-eight. By then some of the largest and best-known American corporations had pulled out, including Eastman Kodak, Ford, General Motors, Coca-Cola, Corning Glass, IBM, Dow Chemical, and Newmont Mining. (Mobil, the largest American company in South Africa, and Goodyear followed in the first half of 1989.) Out of a total of 284 U.S. firms operating in South Africa in December 1984, only 136 remained by July 1988.[49]

Anti-apartheid activism continued and included a mixture of old and new tactics. Shareholder resolutions urging withdrawal by U.S. firms remained at approximately the level they had reached during the height of the sanctions campaign. An investment newsletter reported in November 1988 that "shareholder activism on social issues is not abating. . . . All the publicly held companies that are in South Africa are getting resolutions."[50]

The impact of the campaign was indicated by the reaction of money market managers. For example, global portfolio managers controlling U.S. pension funds invested abroad began to use specially prepared indices offering clients options that avoided companies with South African ties. Mutual funds were also affected. Investors were advised to "get out" of holdings involving South African securities. The "risk of loss is too great to ignore," reported a private newsletter on mutuals. "Sell now and switch to a fund with little or no South African exposure." The advice was prompted by legislation in Congress that would have made it illegal for U.S. citizens—and mutual funds—to hold South African securities. The measure passed the House of Representatives but failed in the Senate.

Nevertheless, the threat of the legislation worried investors and encouraged securities managers to play it safe. David Hauck of the Investor Responsibility Research Center (IRRC) in Washington, D.C., summed up the situation toward the end of 1988. "The estimates of the value of funds under some kind of South African restriction are $30 billion to $40 billion, or one percent to two percent of the value of the U.S. equity market," he noted.[51] This was a small percentage of total U.S. investment capital. However, it represented a significant financial loss for South Africa, which since 1985 had become a capital exporting country.

Demonstrations and boycotts against firms remaining in South Africa also continued. The Free South Africa Movement, for example, launched a consumer boycott against Shell gas stations and products across the country. Shell, an Anglo-Dutch company, is heavily involved in South Africa. FSAM strategists considered it a justifiable target, and the boycott would not threaten American jobs. The campaign, however, did not generate widespread support, possibly because it focused on a foreign corporation in which Americans were not directly involved.

Another tactic went beyond firms with direct holdings in South Africa to encompass all U.S. companies with franchise, licensing or management agreements in that country. Many of the firms that were selling their operations in South Africa maintained a foothold there through licensing and franchising arrangements. Anti-apartheid activists redirected their efforts toward these companies, making it clear that the simple act of disinvestment—the disposal of a company's equity in South Africa—was not enough.

The methods used against companies that maintained South African ties included purging investment portfolios of stocks in firms doing business in South Africa, withdrawing funds from banks with South African ties, and barring public agencies from procuring goods and services from firms connected with South Africa. For instance, Kohlberg Kravis Roberts and Co., which won a major takeover battle to acquire RJR Nabisco in 1988, announced the sale of its South African subsidiaries after the state legislatures of Massachusetts and Michigan withdrew $135 million from a Kohlberg fund used to finance the takeover bid. These "people's sanctions" campaigns resulted in a variety of punitive actions against companies with South African ties by twenty-three states, nineteen counties, and seventy-nine cities by the end of 1988.[52]

Legislation by state and local governments preventing companies involved in South Africa from bidding for public service contracts was perhaps the activists' most effective tactic and sometimes had significant results. Elimination from the bidding process directly limited corporations' domestic sales, reduced their market share, and depreciated the value of their stock. Motorola, once South Africa's leading supplier of electronics and communications equipment, had long resisted shareholder efforts to stop sales to the South African military and police. But the company reversed its stand in 1988, indicating it would end all sales to South Africa when its distribution agreement expired in 1990. The reason was that Metropolitan Dade County, Florida, the largest urban area in the southeast, had passed selective purchasing legislation excluding companies that retained licensing agreements in South Africa from bidding for contracts. By ending its South African business, Motorola dealt itself back into a profitable domestic market.[53]

The results of the continuing activism were seen in numerous other ways. San Francisco passed legislation prohibiting meetings between San Francisco officials and representatives of the South African government, the first such legislation in the United States. The new law was publicized by the city with a billboard campaign financed by Bay Area lawyers. San Francisco also declared apartheid "a crime against humanity."

When Johannesburg's mayor invited the mayor of St. Paul, Minnesota, to travel to South Africa, the American official turned down the invitation. St. Paul prided itself on having helped delay the forced removal of the residents of Lawaaikamp, a South African black township due for demolition. A delegation from St. Paul had lobbied Congress, the South African embassy, and the State Department; it paid for a half-page advertisement in a South African newspaper; and it held church services simultaneously with those in the South African township. Taped messages were exchanged between residents of the two cities. This was all part of a sister-city strategy sponsored by the United States–South Africa Sister Community Project that began in 1988. Berkeley, California, and Oukasie, another black township protesting forced removal and rent hikes, also established a sister community project. Temporary reprieves were achieved for the black townships in both instances.

Efforts such as these gave activists at the local level opportunities to reinforce federal sanctions and to express their opposition to apartheid in a direct fashion. Activists wanted to send "a message to the South African government that we are still watching even though there is virtually a total media blackout."[54]

In Congress, liberals interested in South Africa remained active but recorded few successes. On September 30, 1987, a bipartisan group of thirty-three congressmen and senators, made up of seventeen Republicans and sixteen Democrats, sent a letter to President Reagan to recommend "stronger sanctions" against South Africa "in the absence of significant progress during the last twelve months towards ending the system of apartheid." A press conference was held, together with representatives of the United Mine Workers of America, TransAfrica, the Washington Office on Africa, and the Lawyers Committee for Equal Rights Under Law. But their call elicited a cool response. The president issued a report, as required by the CAAA, in which he agreed that no significant progress had been made toward ending apartheid and stated that the "cycle of violence and counter-violence between the South African government and its opponents has, if anything, gotten worse." Reagan concluded, however, that economic sanctions had not been effective and that further measures would be counterproductive.

The liberals had better results in December 1987, when Congressman Charles Rangel (D–New York) introduced legislation, tacked on to the FY 1988 Deficit Reduction Finance Bill, that denied U.S. firms in South Africa the right to deduct South African taxes from their U.S. taxes. Similar to the measure enacted earlier by conservatives to penalize American companies operating in Angola, the Rangel Amendment, as it came to be known, was passed by both houses. The measure significantly reduced the profit margins of corporations that decided to stay in South Africa. When Mobil announced its withdrawal from South Africa in early 1989, it cited the Rangel Amendment as one of the major reasons for its decision.

Eight months after the passage of the amendment, a bill calling for a virtual economic embargo was introduced by Congressman Ronald Dellums (D–California). The House passed the measure by 244-to-132 votes. A Senate version won approval on a party-line vote of 10–9 in the Senate Foreign Relations Committee but did not reach the floor of the Senate.

The bipartisan cohesion that had produced the CAAA was breaking down, particularly in the Senate. While the Democrats had recaptured control of the Senate in the 1986 midterm elections, in 1988 they lost the support of Senator Weicker, a key liberal Republican who was defeated in the elections. But even more important, many moderate senators—Democrats as well as Republicans—were cautious about taking further measures. Contradictory messages were coming out of South Africa about the impact of existing sanctions, South Africa was out of the news, a presidential election loomed in November, and Crocker's southern African negotiations were in a delicate stage. The Dellums bill consequently failed to make further progress.

The 1988 presidential campaign, in which Jesse Jackson's candidacy seemed certain to refocus attention on South Africa, failed to revive the issue. Jackson, after losing the Democratic primary to Michael Dukakis, helped shape the party's platform on southern Africa. The document declared South Africa a "terrorist state" and called for imposing comprehensive sanctions, ending U.S. aid to UNITA, and establishing diplomatic relations with the Angolan government. The Republican platform reaffirmed the outlines of the Reagan administration's policy and strongly opposed sanctions.

The only mention of southern Africa in the presidential debates between Dukakis and George Bush was the latter's passing reference to progress being made in the Angolan–Namibian negotiations. Both presidential candidates had reason to avoid the issue. Dukakis did not stress sanctions, seemingly for fear of being accused of caving in to Jackson's demands, a perception that could have cost him white votes in the South. Bush opposed sanctions; but he, too, did not seem anxious to call attention to the issue for fear of being too closely associated with an unpopular policy that could cost him black and other votes. Thus, each candidate distanced himself from his party's position on South Africa. In doing so, they mirrored the ambivalence in U.S. policy and the lack of public consensus. The sensitivity of race as a political issue in American politics—the central factor

that makes South Africa an emotive foreign policy dilemma—
seemed to have driven South Africa off the agenda of the 1988
presidential campaign.

A Regional Breakthrough

When the Angolan government broke off negotiations with the
United States in early 1986, following the Reagan administration's
decision to arm UNITA, the prospect of a resolution of the linked
problems of Namibia's independence and the removal of the Cubans
from Angola seemed remote. By the end of 1987, even top administration officials had concluded that U.S. diplomacy in southern
Africa had reached an impasse. Yet, with barely a month of President Reagan's final term left, two interlocking accords were signed
by Angola, Cuba, and South Africa. The ceremony, presided over by
Secretary of State Shultz and witnessed approvingly by a Soviet
deputy foreign minister, brought Chester Crocker's eight-year diplomatic quest to a triumphant conclusion.

There was no single reason for this unexpected outcome.
Rather, a fortuitous mesh of strategic, political, military, and economic conditions made success possible. These included (1) a
change in the U.S.-Soviet relationship that produced cooperation
instead of confrontation in southern Africa; (2) a shift in the balance
of military power in the region, largely as the result of Cuba's
decision to increase its military commitment to Angola and use its
forces more aggressively; (3) rising economic costs for all the warring parties; and (4) the realization by the combatants that they were
fighting an unwinnable war.

The first hint of movement came in March 1987, when Congo-
lese President Denis Sassou-Nguesso, who was later to play an
important middleman's role in the negotiations, sent a message
to the Reagan administration saying that he believed the Angolans
were ready to resume talks. This prompted Crocker to meet with
the Angolan government in Brazzaville in April for "talks about
talks." But the Angolans were also preparing to fight and were
in the process of planning a massive conventional assault against
UNITA. Thus began a diplomatic marathon that led its participants
through many twists and turns, across several continents, and finally
ended at the United Nations in New York City twenty months
later.

In July Crocker went to Luanda for further discussions, but the administration concluded that the Angolans had not shifted significantly from the *plataforma* (position) they had presented to the United States in November 1984, which promised a phased withdrawal of Cuban troops from southern Angola and included a pledge of total Cuban withdrawal at an unspecified future date. In return, the Angolans wanted a total South African withdrawal from the country, an end to Pretoria's support of UNITA, and the implementation of the UN independence plan for Namibia. Crocker, who was looking for an Angolan commitment to a total Cuban withdrawal but did not get it, called the talks "a waste of time."

Meanwhile, the Angolan offensive against UNITA was under way. Soviet military planners were closely involved. However, the Cubans, who disagreed with both the strategy and tactics of the campaign, distanced themselves from it.

It was at this point, in July 1987, that the U.S. administration received an indirect message from Fidel Castro saying that Cuba wanted to participate in the negotiations on a formal basis. The State Department replied that the matter could be acted on only if a request for Cuban participation came from the Angolans. Luanda gave a positive response within seventy-two hours. But State Department officials dealing with Latin American affairs, who were strongly anti-Castro, temporarily blocked Cuban involvement in the negotiations.

Heavy fighting in southeastern Angola shifted the focus to the battlefield. In the fall of 1987, Angola's forces were repulsed trying to cross the Lomba River and capture Mavinga as South Africa came to UNITA's support with several thousand troops, fighter aircraft, and long-range artillery. Encouraged by their success, UNITA and South African forces advanced to lay siege to Cuito Cuanavale, a strategic Angolan forward base and airfield.

Gillian Gunn, a Washington-based analyst, pieced together what happened next:

Angola's President José Eduardo dos Santos responded to the military emergency by meeting with Cuba's Fidel Castro on November 7. The two apparently decided upon a new strategy. Additional Cubans would be sent to Angola. They would be experienced, mature troops rather than the garrison forces normally supplied, and they would take a role in front-line combat rather than being restricted to logistical support operations as previously. In December 1987, for the first time since the mid-1970s, large numbers of Cuban troops moved into southern Angola. One unit went to relieve Cuito Cuanavale, while another continued south toward the Namibian border.[55]

The 15,000 new Cuban troops, well equipped and heavily armed, brought the total in Angola to approximately fifty thousand, the highest number since 1975. Over the course of the next few months, a combined force of Cubans, Angolans, and Namibians established a 270-mile front within twenty miles of the Namibian border. This expansion of Cuba's military role produced a critical turning point in the thirteen-year-old conflict and in the negotiations.

In response to heightened military tensions and Crocker's urging, Secretary of State Shultz decided in January 1988 to overrule the objections of the anti-Cuban faction in the State Department and admit Cuba to the negotiations, provided it came as part of the Angolan delegation. Crocker flew to Luanda the same month and, after meeting with the Angolans and Cubans, announced that the two parties had for the first time agreed to a total withdrawal of the Cuban forces from Angola as part of an overall agreement. Crocker termed this step a "milestone," but a South African spokesman in Washington discounted the news, saying that nothing new had happened. Parallel discussions between the United States and the Soviet Union indicated that the latter was serious in helping the parties reach a settlement.

While Crocker was breaking new ground in Angola, Franz Josef Strauss, the Bavarian leader and a trusted friend of South Africa, visited Pretoria on his own initiative and informed President Botha that Moscow appeared to have concluded that no military solution was possible in Angola and that the Soviets would be prepared to support negotiations.[56] Then, in February, Mikhail Gorbachev announced that the Soviet Union was going to withdraw all its troops from Afghanistan on the basis of a UN accord that could be a model for other regional conflicts.

In March, Foreign Minister Roelof Botha called for talks, proposing that UNITA and the South African-backed internal government in Namibia participate. The Angolans put forward a plan for a Cuban withdrawal over a period of four years. Crocker met Foreign Minister Botha in Geneva to convey the Angolan offer, but the South Africans still did not seem impressed by what Crocker considered a significant change in the Angolan position. Defiantly, President Botha, in an interview in the *Washington Times* of March 14, 1988, said that South Africa would stay in Angola until the Cubans left, making no mention of Namibia.

Shortly thereafter, Defense Minister Magnus Malan, apparently acting on the information provided by Franz Josef Strauss and taking a cue from Gorbachev, made a public offer to the Soviet Union. Using the Afghanistan model, he said that South Africa would withdraw from Angola if the Cubans went home and if the Soviet Union would accept a nonaligned Angolan government based on reconciliation between the MPLA and UNITA. The Soviets dismissed the offer, saying that Angola and Afghanistan were entirely different.

Finally, in May 1988 formal negotiations between Angola, Cuba, and South Africa began in London. Significantly, each delegation included top military officers as well as diplomats. Crocker acted as convener and chairperson. A senior Soviet official, present as an "observer," played a supportive role behind the scenes. Neither SWAPO nor UNITA was an official participant, but both were regularly briefed by their allies. This set the pattern for the meetings to follow.

Meanwhile, South Africa pursued a second diplomatic track by arranging to meet with the Angolans in Brazzaville shortly after the London talks, a tactic that took the Americans by surprise. A senior Reagan administration official interpreted this as a last-ditch attempt by South Africa to bypass American mediation. Pretoria's objective, he speculated, was to threaten Angola with additional military pressure, forcing it to negotiate a separate deal that left Namibia out of the package.[57] The Brazzaville meeting did not produce any agreements, but it alerted the Cubans to the possibility that the South Africans might open up a new front to force Angola's hand. Accordingly, Cuba strengthened its forces along the Namibian border.

In late June, delegations from Angola, Cuba, and South Africa met again, this time in Cairo. The mood was combative and tense, but the participants agreed on the need for a set of principles as a basis for the overall agreement. Still, the critical arena remained the battlefield. The day after the Cairo meeting, an Angolan-Cuban force clashed with South African military units around the Calueque Dam, which supplies water to Namibia, in southwestern Angola. To the northeast, the siege of Cuito Cuanavale continued. During the fighting, the South Africans suffered what was for them relatively high white casualties and had two out of twelve operational fighter aircraft shot down.

The most significant result of the clashes, however, was South Africa's loss of air supremacy over southwestern Angola. Angolan aircraft began overflying South African military facilities in Namibia, raising concern in Pretoria that Angolan-Cuban forces might cross the border and substantially escalate the war. South Africa did not retaliate on the battlefield but it called up its reserves. Defense Minister Malan demanded that the United States act: "South Africa can rightly expect Dr. Crocker to do something concrete about the situation. . . . The build-up of troops is contrary to the spirit and intention of the negotiations." Crocker himself kept silent, but a spokesperson for the State Department said, "It is for the parties to decide whether they wish to bring negotiations to a successful conclusion or whether they wish to pursue illusory military solutions."[58]

Within South Africa, the war was becoming a controversial political issue. The Dutch Reformed church, the spiritual home of most Afrikaners, questioned the government's strategy. "We have to ask ourselves if it is, any longer, right for South Africa to be in Angola," *Die Kerkbode,* the official journal of the church, commented in August 1988. Combat deaths were fueling the anticonscription campaign among young whites and worrying leaders of the ruling National Party, which was facing important municipal elections later in the year. South Africa was also under economic pressure. The Reserve Bank, the country's central bank, warned that South Africa would have difficulty meeting its foreign debt payments. President Botha acknowledged that the country faced a $4 billion loss of capital over the next five years.[59] "If anything is driving home the need to look seriously at the peace agreement, it is economics," stated a South African academic. "In this sense, sanctions contribute to the negotiations because the government has to cut expenses."[60] At the end of the year, the *Weekly Mail,* a South African newspaper, wrote, "This was the year financial sanctions struck home."

A shift in the decision-making process within the government also appeared to take place. "In Pretoria the influence of the military was giving way to that of the Foreign Office, as the government seemed to realize the geopolitical limits of its power," wrote John Marcum in an assessment of the year's events.[61]

If Cuba's expansion of its military role in Angola in late 1987 was the first critical turning point, South Africa's decision to withdraw from that country and begin serious negotiations over Namibia's independence in the summer of 1988 was the second. Indications of Pretoria's changed attitude became clear at a meeting in New York in July 1988. Angola, Cuba, and South Africa developed a document entitled "General Principles for a Peaceful Settlement in Southwestern Africa." The principles were deliberately vague; but they included, under the rubric of respect for territorial integrity and noninterference in internal affairs, reciprocal tacit concessions suggesting that South Africa would cease to aid UNITA and Angola would close the ANC's bases as part of the general settlement.

The principles also gave the talks a momentum that led to a meeting in Geneva in early August and resulted in a cessation of fighting in Angola. The South Africans agreed to withdraw from Angola by the end of August; Cuba and Angola agreed to ensure that SWAPO forces would be kept north of the 16th parallel, roughly one hundred miles away from the Namibian border; November 1, 1988, was set as the date for implementation of the UN plan for Namibia's independence.

In Angola, South African and UNITA forces began to withdraw, ending the long, bitter siege of Cuito Cuanavale. The last South African units pulled back into Namibia ahead of schedule at the end of August. The situation was very different from five months earlier, when President Botha had pledged that South Africa would stay in Angola until the Cubans left.

More talks were planned in order to develop a timetable for Cuban troop withdrawal, the main problem at this stage. Several meetings were held in Brazzaville, New York, and Geneva in the following months. There was a certain amount of posturing, considerable horse-trading, and some hesitation during the run-up to the American presidential elections while the parties tried to calculate whether the outcome would work to their advantage.

Final agreement was reached on December 13 with the signing of the Protocol of Brazzaville, which committed the belligerents to sign two interlocking peace treaties and established the Angolan-Cuban–South African Joint Commission to monitor implementation. The United States and the Soviet Union were given observer status in the commission. The terms of the final agreement set a new implementation date of April 1, 1989, for the UN Namibia plan; elections would be held on November 1, 1989; and the country was expected to become independent several months later, although this was not spelled out in the agreement. Cuban troops would leave Angola in a phased withdrawal that would be completed by mid-1991.

The treaties were signed at a ceremony in the United Nations on December 22, 1988. (See Appendix E.) One was a tripartite agreement between Angola, Cuba, and South Africa, providing for the independence of Namibia under the UN plan; the other was a bilateral agreement between Angola and Cuba detailing the Cuban withdrawal schedule from Angola. The United States, as mediator, was not a signatory but, together with the Soviet Union, became a guarantor of the accords.

Crocker, who had become more used to criticism than praise during his time in office, received almost universal approval for his role in the negotiations. Some conservative groups in the United States opposed the accords, faulting them for favoring the Cubans, promoting a Soviet-dominated government in Namibia, and leaving UNITA out in the cold. But for the most part, the agreements were widely applauded.

David Ottaway, writing in the *Washington Post* on December 23, 1988, noted Crocker's endurance. "Starting in April 1981, when [he] made his first trip to southern Africa, the U.S. mediator had been waiting patiently for the right alignment of local, regional and international events—like the planets lining up for some rare astronomical happening as he himself put it—to clinch a deal." Anatoly Adamishin, the Soviet deputy foreign minister and "Crocker's reliable behind-the-scenes partner," according to Chas. Freeman, Crocker's senior deputy,[62] praised the assistant secretary's "brilliant role."[63] Randall Robinson of TransAfrica, who had strongly criticized constructive engagement but praised Crocker's stand on Mozambique, acknowledged that Crocker deserved "kudos for a major effort" and that the settlement, while containing uncertainties, represented "a significant achievement."[64] The *Wall Street Journal* wrote in an editorial on December 14, 1988, that the successful outcome was "one of the most significant foreign policy achievements of the Reagan Administration."

Conclusion

In the final analysis, constructive engagement, a highly complex and nuanced policy, will be associated with a major success in its regional diplomacy and a major failure in its South African strategy.

Paradoxically, the Reagan administration, which propounded a strong anti-Soviet line and was criticized for racial insensitivity, helped end both the cold war and colonialism in southern Africa. This was achieved by U.S.-mediated treaties that removed the Cubans from Angola and set Namibia on the path to independence. A convergence of international and regional dynamics, rather than policy, created the conditions for this outcome. Crocker's tenacity, despite repeated setbacks, was also a factor. "Circumstances having become propitious," John Marcum observed, "Chester Crocker's persistence paid off."[65]

In his regional diplomacy, Crocker demonstrated considerable flexibility, especially in the final year of the Reagan administration. Although he shared many of the geopolitical concerns of the administration and its conservative supporters, he adapted his vision and his tactics when the global and regional climate changed significantly. Having entered office with sympathy for what he perceived as the South African government's legitimate fears in the region, he grew increasingly skeptical as South Africa's regional strategy became clear. Eventually, he came to realize that South Africa's military attacks on its neighbors went well beyond the needs of legitimate defense. They resulted in greater instability in the region, which created opportunities for the Soviet Union and damaged the interests of the United States and its Western allies.

In his formulation of constructive engagement, Crocker ruled out punitive actions against South Africa and consistently opposed such measures throughout the Reagan years. But, in pursuit of an Angolan-Namibian settlement, he took advantage of the pressures applied by others as he struggled to handle Pretoria's aggression and find leverage in the negotiations. For instance, Crocker turned a blind eye to Castro's decision to escalate Cuba's military role in Angola—an action that produced the critical pressure needed to persuade Pretoria to negotiate seriously.

By contrast, the domestic failure of the administration's South Africa policy, culminating in the passage of the Comprehensive Anti-Apartheid Act (CAAA), resulted largely from Crocker's misreading of South African as well as U.S. political dynamics and from his unwillingness to reassess his policy when these miscalculations became evident. He based his policy on questionable premises about President Botha's domestic agenda and the character of the South African government. Overcompensating for what he considered excessive rhetorical hostility toward Pretoria by the Carter administration, Crocker tried to identify with South Africa's strategic interests, particularly its anticommunism, and to empathize with white fears. Stressing persuasion over pressure, he signaled in advance that there would be no significant penalties for lack of cooperation.

Crocker mistakenly assumed that Botha's streamlining of the government bureaucracy and his modest reforms were inaugurating a period of political modernization leading to fundamental change, including political rights for blacks. However, Botha's bureaucratic policies were aimed at consolidating personal power, and his social and economic reforms, while more than cosmetic, were based on traditional racial and ethnic criteria that entrenched rather than dismantled apartheid. The 1984 constitution, for example, excluded the African majority, triggering the black uprising.

The military component of the government, which exerted an unprecedented degree of influence under Botha, also played a markedly different role from the one Crocker had expected. Instead of being the band of reformist "modernizing patriots" he had suggested, South Africa's military elites revealed themselves to be hard-line on regional and internal issues. During the 1980s they launched the most extensive and sustained attacks on South Africa's neighbors and imposed the harshest crackdown on internal dissent in South African history.

Crocker also underestimated black power in South Africa and failed to consider the possibility that blacks could mount a revolutionary challenge that would plunge the country into crisis and generate an international outcry. Stressing the power of the state and the fragmentation of black politics, Crocker was neither prepared for the scope, duration, and intensity of the 1984–86 black revolt nor ready to change his strategy in light of this development. His unwillingness to take a strong position against Pretoria's repression made the administration appear inflexible and unsympathetic to black South African anger and aspirations.

Similarly, Crocker failed to anticipate the extent and power of the political opposition that this issue generated in the United States. His lack of sensitivity in handling Congress, the press, and anti-apartheid activists alienated many of his supporters as well as his critics. Fundamentally, widespread public opposition, a factor never previously important in U.S. policy toward South Africa, was the final undoing of constructive engagement.

President Reagan, however, must share a large part of the responsibility for the public repudiation of the administration's policy. His attitude toward blacks, shown in part by his lack of consultation with the Congressional Black Caucus, his offhand comments that distorted the facts and showed an instinctive sympathy for the South African government, and his refusal in 1986 to compromise with congressional leaders of his own party all combined to produce a showdown that enabled Congress not only to condemn the policy but also to step in and remake it.

Beyond the policy concerns of the Reagan years, several important changes occurred in the nature of U.S.–South African relations during this period that have long-term implications. The United States became more involved, not only in South Africa, but in the region as a whole. Congressional support for sanctions, grassroots pressure for disinvestment, the expansion of economic assistance to black South Africans, bipartisan support for aid to anti-apartheid groups in South Africa, the continued search by liberal activists for ways to support black South Africans in their quest to dismantle apartheid, military aid to UNITA, the State Department's steady support of the Mozambican government, and the growing interest of a cross-section of the Washington policy community in aiding the Southern African Development Coordination Conference (SADCC)—though sometimes appearing to be at cross purposes— are all indicators of increased U.S. involvement. As a result, some old taboos have been broken, constraints inherent in the old policies are gone, and new policy actions are available.

Mikhail Gorbachev's "new thinking" and the unprecedented U.S.-Soviet cooperation over the Angolan-Namibian peace accords brought an end to the cold war in southern Africa. Important changes in Soviet thinking on South Africa itself were also evident. These included a reduced emphasis on the armed struggle and revolutionary violence, a clear desire to preserve South Africa's economy, and talk of protecting white minority rights.

It may take some time to determine whether the United States and the Soviet Union can work together on other regional issues and on South Africa itself. Even if cooperation is achieved, there is a limit to the superpowers' influence; they cannot impose a settlement on the people of the region or solve South Africa's internal problems. But the removal of the Soviet Union as a hostile regional competitor—whether or not it becomes a regional partner—is bound to have a significant impact on U.S.–South African relations and on South Africa's relations with its neighbors.

The debate over constructive engagement also heightened public awareness of South Africa and the region. Stereotypical perceptions of black passivity and racial monoliths were, to some extent, replaced by more realistic perceptions of South Africa's political and social complexities. The stamina and passion of black protest in South Africa surprised many Americans, as did the serious political divisions within both the white and black communities. The problems of the other states in the region and South Africa's impact on them also became widely recognized.

Perhaps the most fundamental change that occurred during the Reagan years, however, concerns Americans' perceptions of South Africa. Traditionally, South Africa was viewed as a remote issue and was cast largely in terms of the United States' strategic, political, and economic interests. But, as a result of the debate during the Reagan years, South Africa will have greater visibility and importance in the next decade, and it will be seen by the public overwhelmingly as a human rights issue.

This shift is due partly to the changing nature of U.S. interests in South Africa. Strategic concerns have eased since Gorbachev came to power and the American economic presence has been reduced as a result of sanctions and disinvestment. But there is a deeper reason behind this transformation that predates Gorbachev and sanctions. Apartheid has become a domestic as well as a foreign policy issue. It touches not only the 12 percent of the U.S. population that traces its ancestry to Africa, but raises for all Americans the issue of race, one of the most controversial, emotive, and powerful forces in American politics. Rightly or wrongly, many Americans now appear to feel that the position the United States takes on South Africa reflects America's most basic values. In this sense, U.S. relations with South Africa have crossed a new threshold.

THE

WEEKLY MAIL

PRICES: JOHANNESBURG, PRETORIA & REEF R1,00 (plus 12c GST) | ELSEWHERE IN SA R1,12 (excl. GST)

Volume 2, Number 24. FRIDAY JUNE 20 to THURSDAY JUNE 26, 1986

THE PAPER FOR A CHANGING SOUTH AFRICA

WE'RE BACK ON THE STREETS! The paper that was seized last week will be on sale as usual from today

FRONT PAGE COMMENT

Our lawyers tell us we can say almost nothing critical about the Emergency

But we'll try:

PIK BOTHA, the Minister of Foreign Affairs, told US television audiences this week that the South African press remained free.

We hope that ██████████████████, ████████████████████████████, was listening.

They considered our publication subversive.
- If it is subversive to speak out against ███████, we plead guilty.
- If it is subversive to express concern about ████████, we plead guilty.
- If it is subversive to believe that there are better routes to peace than the ███████████, we plead guilty.

● To PAGE 2

RESTRICTED ▓▓▓▓ Reports on these pages have been censored to comply with Emergency regulations

---

South African newspaper's response to state of emergency
(International Defense & Aid Fund for Southern Africa)

Notes

REAGAN'S FIRST TERM: THE RISE OF CONSTRUCTIVE
ENGAGEMENT

1. William H. Lewis, "United States Response to Inter-African Regional Problems and Prospects," in *Beyond Constructive Engagement: United States Foreign Policy Toward Africa,* ed. Elliot P. Skinner (New York: Paragon House Publishers, 1986), 99.

2. "New U.S. Policy on South Africa: State Department Documents Uncover Developing Alliance," *TransAfrica News Report* 1, no. 10 (Special Edition, August 1981), 3.

3. Chester A. Crocker, "The U.S. Policy Process and South Africa," in *The American People and South Africa: Publics, Elites, and Policymaking Processes,* ed. Alfred O. Hero, Jr., and John Barratt (Lexington, Mass.: D. C. Heath and Company, Lexington Books, 1981), 143.

4. Chester A. Crocker, "South Africa: Strategy for Change," *Foreign Affairs* 59, no. 2 (Winter 1980–81): 346.

5. Crocker, "South Africa: Strategy for Change," 337, 345.

6. "New U.S. Policy on South Africa," 6.

7. Chester A. Crocker, "African Policy in the 1980s," *The Washington Quarterly* 3, no. 3 (Summer 1980): 85.

8. Crocker, "South Africa: Strategy for Change," 337, 338.

9. "New U.S. Policy on South Africa," 3.

10. Ibid.

11. Ibid.

12. Crocker, "South Africa: Strategy for Change," 341, 342.

13. Crocker, "South Africa: Strategy for Change," 327, 345, 351.

14. Secretary of State's Advisory Committee on South Africa, *A U.S. Policy Toward South Africa* (Washington, D.C.: The Department of State, 1987), vi.

15. William Finnegan, "Coming Apart Over Apartheid: The Story Behind the Republicans' Split on South Africa," *Mother Jones,* April/May 1986, 40.

16. "New U.S. Policy on South Africa," 3–4.

17. Simon Jenkins, "Destabilisation in Southern Africa," *The Economist*, 16–22 July 1983, 28.

18. "Agreement Near on Ending Namibia War, American Officials Say," *Washington Post*, 14 July 1982.

19. Remarks by Crocker in discussions with African specialists at seminars and professional briefings in Washington, D.C., during this period.

20. Ken Flower, *Serving Secretly: Rhodesia's CIO Chief on Record* (Alberton, South Africa: Galago, 1987), 262.

21. Revealed in RENAMO documents captured at Gorongosa, Mozambique. Nel made the trip on June 8, 1985. See David Martin and Phyllis Johnson, "Mozambique: Victims of Apartheid," in *Frontline Southern Africa: Destructive Engagement*, ed. Phyllis Johnson and David Martin (New York: Four Walls Eight Windows, 1988), 32–34. The South African government later acknowledged Nel's trip, claiming that it was necessary in order to facilitate peace talks between RENAMO and the Mozambican government.

22. John C. Whitehead, "The Potential Impact of Imposing Sanctions Against South Africa," statement before the Senate Committee on Foreign Relations, Washington, D.C., 22 June 1988.

23. Interview with Stephen Weissman, 11 May 1989.

24. Interview with Philip L. Christenson, 12 May 1989.

25. Interview with Timothy Bork, director, Office of Project Development, U.S. Agency for International Development (USAID), 11 May 1989. Also, interview with Mike Feldstein, USAID official, 12 May 1989. For more details on the debate, see House Committee on Foreign Affairs, *U.S. Educational Assistance in South Africa: Critical Policy Issues*, Report of a Staff Study Mission to South Africa, 21–28 August 1982, 97th Cong., 2d sess., 30 December 1982; Subcommittee on Africa of the House Committee on Foreign Affairs, *Hearings and Markup, Foreign Assistance Legislation for Fiscal Years 1986–87 (Part 7)*, 99th Cong., 1st sess., 5, 7, and 19 March 1985; and Lawyers Committee for Human Rights, *United States Policy Toward South Africa*, 1988 Project Series No. 1, Human Rights and U.S. Foreign Policy (New York, 1989).

REAGAN'S SECOND TERM: CONSTRUCTIVE ENGAGEMENT UNDER FIRE

26. Steven McDonald, "Washington Pauses to Reassess the South African Sanctions Issue," *CSIS Africa Notes*, 20 January 1989, 2.

27. See Anthony Sampson, *Black and Gold: Tycoons, Revolutionaries, and Apartheid* (New York: Pantheon Books, 1987), 42.

28. "South Africa and T.V.: The Coverage Changes," *New York Times*, 29 December 1985.

29. Statement by the Reverend Leon H. Sullivan, 3 June 1987, in Philadelphia.

30. Finnegan, "Coming Apart Over Apartheid," 19.

31. "31 Hill Conservatives Denounce Apartheid," *Washington Times*, 6 December 1984. (The final letter had thirty-five signatures.)

32. Bob Woodward, *Veil: The Secret Wars of the CIA, 1981–87* (New York: Simon & Schuster, Inc., 1987), 426.

33. "Limited Economic Sanctions Imposed on South Africa," *Washington Post*, 10 September 1985.

34. Interviews with government officials confirmed that there was a struggle within the administration over this speech, with Buchanan gaining the upper hand.

35. Simon Barber, "Shadows on the Wall," *Optima*, June 1987, 75.

36. *Congressional Record*, 99th Cong., 2d sess., 15 August 1986, S11868.

37. Pauline H. Baker, "The Sanctions Vote: A G.O.P. Milestone," *New York Times*, 26 August 1986.

38. "Kassebaum Backs Senate Override," *Washington Times*, 1 October 1986.

39. "Shultz Calls U.S. Policy Unchanged," *Washington Post*, 11 January 1987.

40. *Foreign Broadcasting and Information Service*, Sub-Saharan Africa, 14 December 1987.

41. See Laurence I. Barrett, *Gambling with History: Ronald Reagan in the White House* (New York: Penguin Books, 1984), 61.

42. Woodward, *Veil: The Secret Wars of the CIA, 1981–87*, 426.

43. "4 Rebel Units Sign Anti-Soviet Pact: U.S. Conservatives Organize Guerrilla Policy in Angola—Lehrman Has Role," *New York Times*, 6 June 1985.

44. Congress had already blocked Export-Import Bank loans to U.S. firms trading with Angola in October 1984.

45. Interview with Timothy Roemer, foreign policy aide to Senator Dennis DeConcini, 19 May 1989.

46. Angola Task Force members: William Armstrong (R–Colorado), Dale Bumpers (D–Arkansas), Alfonse D'Amato (R–New York), Dennis DeConcini (D–Arizona), Bob Graham (D–Florida), Charles E. Grassley (R–Iowa), Ernest F. Hollings (D–South Carolina), Gordon J. Humphrey (R–New Hampshire), David Kemp Karnes (R–Nebraska), Robert Kasten (R–Wisconsin), James A. McClure (R–Idaho), William Proxmire (D–Wisconsin), Richard C. Shelby (D–Alabama), Steven D. Symms (R–Idaho), Pete Wilson (R–California).

47. Robert Mugabe, "Struggle for Southern Africa," *Foreign Affairs* 66, no. 2 (Winter 1987–88): 318.

48. Interview with State Department official, 18 May 1989.

49. Figures from interview with David Hauck, Investor Responsibility Research Center (IRRC), 9 May 1989. Discrepancies between these figures and those found in other sources, or in updated IRRC reports, are due

to different counting methods and to confusion created by mergers, sales to other U.S. firms, and partial disinvestments.

50. Trudy Ring, "Social Issues Remain: S. Africa, N. Ireland on '89 Proxy Agenda," *Pensions and Investment Age,* 28 November 1988, 3.

51. David Hauck, "New Indices Offer South Africa–Free Investment," *Financial Times,* 8 November 1988.

52. Reed Kramer, "Cities and States Pressure Companies," *Africa News,* 20 February 1989, 8; also "When States Divest, Corporations Listen," *Bulletin of Municipal Foreign Policy* 3, no. 2 (Spring 1989): 7.

53. Kramer, "Cities and States Pressure Companies," 8–9.

54. Will Swain, "Bleeding Art: San Francisco Gets Its Message Across," *Bulletin of Municipal Foreign Policy* 3, no. 2 (Spring 1989): 42.

55. Gillian Gunn, "A Guide to the Intricacies of the Angola-Namibia Negotiations," *CSIS Africa Notes,* 8 September 1988, 3.

56. "Strauss Sees Soviet Shift on Angola," *Times* (London), 26 January 1988.

57. Interview with U.S. official, 8 March 1989.

58. Gunn, "Angola-Namibia Negotiations," 11.

59. *Foreign Broadcasting and Information Service,* Sub-Saharan Africa, 22 September 1988.

60. Interview with South African university lecturer, September 1988.

61. John A. Marcum, "Africa: A Continent Adrift," *Foreign Affairs: America and the World 1988* 68, no. 1 (1989): 166.

62. Chas. W. Freeman, "The Angola/Namibia Accords," *Foreign Affairs* 68, no. 3 (Summer 1989): 137.

63. "For Crocker, Accord Was Long Time Coming," *Washington Post,* 14 December 1988.

64. Ibid.

CONCLUSION

65. Marcum, "Africa: A Continent Adrift," 167.

Chronology:
United States/South Africa

World War II

South Africa enters war over opposition of Afrikaner nationalists.

1949

United States supports UN resolution referring South Africa to International Court of Justice for failure to comply with UN trusteeship plan for South-West Africa (Namibia).

1950

South African government, pressured by parliamentary opposition, sends fighter squadron to Korea.

1952

Activists in U.S. civil rights movement organize group in sympathy with African National Congress Defiance Campaign in South Africa. United States abstains on apartheid resolution in UN General Assembly.

1957

United States and South Africa begin ten-year program on peaceful uses of atomic energy.

1958

United States abandons policy of abstention and for first time supports a mild UN General Assembly anti-apartheid resolution expressing "regret and concern" over South Africa's racial policies. United States establishes Bureau of African Affairs in State Department; formerly dealt with Africa through European bureau.

1960

April: United States supports first UN Security Council resolution on South Africa, condemning it for the Sharpeville shootings, declaring apartheid a matter of international concern, and establishing a special UN committee on apartheid.

1963

United States imposes unilateral arms embargo against South Africa, effective January 1, 1964, and votes in favor of non-binding UN resolution calling on all countries to do likewise.

1964

U.S. Export-Import Bank stops credits for U.S.–South African trade.

1967

U.S. Navy ships stop using South African ports. Ten-year agreement on peaceful uses of nuclear energy renewed for another decade.

1969

National Security Study Memorandum 39 (NSSM 39), prepared under National Security Adviser Henry Kissinger, forms basis for Nixon administration's policy of "communication" with South Africa. U.S. arms embargo relaxed.

1971

Congressional Black Caucus calls on U.S. government to isolate South Africa.

1974

April: Portuguese coup raises the priority of southern Africa among U.S. policymakers.

1976

January: Clark Amendment bars further U.S. aid to any of the factions in Angola (repealed in 1985). **April:** Key speech by Kissinger in Lusaka, Zambia, lays out U.S. policy priorities in southern Africa, focusing on Rhodesia.

1977

March 1: The Reverend Leon Sullivan introduces a "Statement of Principles" for U.S. businesses in South Africa. **May:** U.S. Vice President Walter Mondale meets South African Prime Minister John Vorster in Vienna and endorses majority rule in South Africa. **August:** United States condemns South Africa for allegedly planning atomic test in Kalahari Desert. **October 19:** United States recalls ambassador and tightens arms embargo after South African government cracks down on black opposition. **November 4:** United

States supports UN Security Council resolution making 1963 voluntary arms embargo mandatory.

1978

September 29: UN Security Council Resolution 435 endorses plan, brokered by Carter administration and backed by Western Contact Group (United States, Britain, France, West Germany, Canada), calling for a cease-fire in Namibia and UN-supervised elections leading to independence in 1979.

1980

November: Ronald Reagan elected president.

1981

January: South Africa pulls out of Geneva Conference convened to implement UN plan for Namibia. **March 4:** President Reagan says United States should back Pretoria while South Africa tries to solve its problems; Prime Minister Pieter W. Botha calls statement realistic policy shift. **June:** United States links Namibian independence to withdrawal of Cuban forces from Angola. **August 31:** United States, citing Cuban presence in Angola, casts solitary veto against UN Security Council resolution condemning South Africa's invasion of Angola.

1982

February 26: United States lifts ban on sale of nonmilitary items to South African police and military.

1983

United States cautiously endorses new South African constitution as "a step in the right direction."

1984

February 16: United States mediates Lusaka Agreement between South Africa and Angola. **March 16:** United States brokers Nkomati Accord between South Africa and Mozambique. **November 21:** Free South Africa Movement launches anti-apartheid campaign with a demonstration outside South African embassy in Washington, D.C. **December 4:** Thirty-five conservative House Republicans send letter to South African ambassador threatening to support sanctions.

1985

June 14: U.S. recalls ambassador from South Africa to protest Pretoria's attacks on neighbors. **July 31:** Chase Manhattan Bank refuses to roll over loans to South Africa; foreign banks follow on September 4, setting off financial crisis in South Africa. **August 15:** Botha delivers "Rubicon" speech. **September 9:** President Reagan's executive order imposes trade and financial sanctions against South Africa, including bar on loans to Pretoria and ban on import of Krugerrands, in move to preempt stronger congressional measures; Sullivan Code made mandatory. **September 19:** President Reagan meets with Mozambican president, Samora Machel.

1986

January 30: President Reagan meets with UNITA leader, Jonas Savimbi; United States agrees to supply arms. **May 23:** United States recalls military attaché and expels South African attaché after South Africa raids alleged African National Congress (ANC) bases in Zimbabwe, Botswana, and Zambia on May 19. **July 18:** University of California decides to divest $3.1 billion from companies doing business with South Africa—largest divestment to date from a college or university. **August 25:** The state of California divests stock worth nearly eleven billion in companies active in South Africa—largest single South Africa-related divestment action at the state or local government level. **October 2:** U.S. Senate overrides Reagan veto on Comprehensive Anti-Apartheid Act (CAAA). **October 15:** Career diplomat Edward J. Perkins confirmed as first black U.S. ambassador to South Africa. **October 20:** General Motors Corporation, the largest U.S. company in South Africa, announces intention to pull out; IBM announces withdrawal next day.

1987

January 28: Oliver Tambo, president of exiled ANC, meets with Secretary of State George Shultz in Washington. **January:** Secretary of State's Advisory Committee on South Africa issues report. **June:** Sullivan calls for total U.S. disinvestment, trade embargo, and break in diplomatic relations with South Africa. **July:** Congress passes Pressler Amendment. **October 2:** In compliance with CAAA, President Reagan reports to Congress that South Africa has not made "significant progress" toward ending apartheid, but opposes additional sanctions. **December 19:** Congress passes Rangel Amendment ending practice of U.S. companies deducting taxes paid in South Africa from their U.S. taxes. Reinforced Cuban troops move toward Namibian border at end of year.

1988

April 19: State Department releases Gersony Report on RENAMO atrocities in Mozambique. **May 3 & 4:** United States, Angola, South Africa, and Cuba begin talks on Angola and Namibia. **June:** South Africans and Angolan-Cuban forces clash at Calueque Dam. **July 20:** Angola, Cuba, and South Africa agree to "Principles for a Peaceful Settlement in Southwestern Africa." **August:** South African troops leave Angola. **December 13:** Brazzaville Protocol signed. **December 22:** Angola, Cuba, and South Africa sign interlocking accords providing for independence of Namibia and the withdrawal of Cuban troops from Angola.

Selected Bibliography:
United States/South Africa

ALBRIGHT, David E. *Soviet Policy Toward Africa Revisited.* CSIS Significant Issues Series, vol. IX, no. 6. Washington, D.C.: Center for Strategic and International Studies, 1987.

BAKER, Pauline H. "Facing Up to Apartheid." *Foreign Policy,* no. 64 (Fall 1986).

CLARIZIO, Linda; CLEMENTS, Bradley; and GEETTER, Erika. "United States Policy Toward South Africa." *Human Rights Quarterly* 11 (1989).

CLOUGH, Michael. "Southern Africa: Challenges and Choices." *Foreign Affairs* 66, no. 5 (Summer 1988).

CROCKER, Chester A. "South Africa: Strategy for Change." *Foreign Affairs* 59, no. 2 (Winter 1980–81).

DE ST. JORRE, John. "South Africa Embattled." *Foreign Affairs: America and the World 1986* 65, no. 3 (1987).

FOLTZ, William J. "United States Policy Toward South Africa: Is One Possible?" in *African Crisis Areas,* edited by Gerard J. Bender, James S. Coleman, and Richard L. Sklar. Berkeley and Los Angeles: University of California Press, 1985.

FREEMAN, Chas. W. "The Angola/Namibia Accords." *Foreign Affairs* 68, no. 3 (Summer 1989).

GORDON, David F. "Southern Africa: Demise of the Centrist Consensus." *SAIS Review* 6, no. 2 (Summer/Fall 1986).

HAUCK, David. *What Happens When U.S. Companies Sell Their South African Operations?* Washington, D.C.: Investor Responsibility Research Center, 1987.

JASTER, Robert S. *South Africa and Its Regional Neighbours: The Dynamics of Regional Conflict.* London: International Institute for Strategic Studies, 1986.

KARIS, Thomas G. "South African Liberation: The Communist Factor." *Foreign Affairs* 65, no. 2 (Winter 1986–87).

KARIS, Thomas G. "United States Policy Toward South Africa." *Southern Africa: The Continuing Crisis,* edited by Gwendolen Carter and Patrick

O'Meara. Bloomington, Ind., and London: Indiana University Press, 1979.

KITCHEN, Helen, and CLOUGH, Michael. *The United States and South Africa: Realities and Red Herrings*. CSIS Significant Issues Series, vol. VI, no. 6. Washington, D.C.: Center for Strategic and International Studies, 1984.

MARCUM, John A. "Africa: A Continent Adrift." *Foreign Affairs: America and the World 1988* 68, no. 1 (1989).

MCDOUGALL, Gay J., ed. *Implementation of the Comprehensive Anti-Apartheid Act of 1986*. A report by the South Africa Project of the Lawyers' Committee for Civil Rights under Law. Washington, D.C.: June 1988.

MINTER, William. "South Africa: Straight Talk on Sanctions." *Foreign Policy*, no. 65 (Winter 1986–87).

U.S. GENERAL ACCOUNTING OFFICE. *South Africa: Trends in Trade, Lending and Investment*. Washington, D.C.: April 1988.

UNGAR, Sanford J., and VALE, Peter. "Why Constructive Engagement Failed." *Foreign Affairs* 64, no. 2 (Winter 1985–86).

Key Events in South African History

B.C.–1902

B.C.: San ("Bushmen") and Khoikhoi ("Hottentots") reside in area now known as South Africa. **A.D. 200–300:** Bantu-speaking African farmers cross Limpopo River and move southward into the eastern part of present-day South Africa. **1488:** Portuguese explorers circumnavigate Cape of Good Hope. **1500–1600:** Africans settle in Transvaal, Orange Free State, Natal, and Eastern Cape. **1652–1795:** Dutch East India Company establishes a station in Cape Peninsula. Dutch, German, and French Huguenot immigrants settle in the Cape and merge to become "Afrikaners" (called "Boers" by the British); slaves imported from East Indies, Madagascar, and other parts of Africa; indigenous San and Khoikhoi die off or are assimilated. **1760:** First "pass laws" introduced when all slaves in Cape required to carry documents designed to control movement of population.

1795–1806: British capture Cape Colony from Dutch in 1795; conquest legalized by treaty in 1806. **1816–28:** Zulu kingdom rises under Shaka. **1820:** Several thousand English immigrants arrive; most settle in Eastern Cape. **1811–78:** Xhosa and British fight frontier wars in Eastern Cape; Xhosa defeated. **1834:** Britain abolishes slavery throughout empire.

1836–40: Afrikaner farmers, rejecting British rule, make "Great Trek" into interior. **1838:** Afrikaners defeat Zulus at battle of Blood River in Natal; event celebrated by Afrikaners annually on December 16 as "Day of the Covenant." **1841:** Lovedale Missionary Institution established in Eastern Cape, first African secondary school. **1843:** Britain annexes Natal. **1852–54:** Britain recognizes South African Republic (Transvaal) and Orange Free State as independent Afrikaner states. **1853:** Nonracial, qualified franchise established in Cape Colony through British influence. In later decades, colonial legislature curtails extension of franchise for Africans, but African voters, around 1900, hold balance of power in a handful of districts. **1860–1911:** Indentured laborers brought from India by British to work on Natal sugar plantations; most settle permanently.

1867: Diamonds discovered north of Cape Colony, near Kimberley. **1877:** Britain annexes Transvaal. **1879:** Zulus defeat British at Isandhlwana.

1880: Britain defeats Zulus at Ulundi and annexes Zululand. **1880–81:** First Anglo–Boer War; Transvaal Afrikaners regain their independence. **1884:** First African-edited newspaper started. **1886:** Gold discovered on the Witwatersrand. **1894:** Natal Indian Congress formed under Mohandas Gandhi. **1898:** Afrikaners defeat Venda, the last independent African kingdom. **1899–1902:** Second Anglo–Boer War ends with Afrikaner defeat; Transvaal and Orange Free State republics become self-governing crown colonies.

1910

Union of South Africa formed as self-governing British dominion with all-white parliament; General Louis Botha, leader of Afrikaner-English coalition and supported by General Jan Smuts, becomes first prime minister.

1912

South African Native National Congress, first national African political movement, founded to overcome ethnic divisions and oppose racial segregation; renamed African National Congress (ANC) in 1923.

1913

Natives Land Act limits land ownership by Africans, 70 percent of total population, to reserves, equaling about 7 percent of land.

1914

Afrikaners form National Party under General J. B. M. Hertzog to oppose Botha and Smuts. South African armed forces fight in World War I on side of Britain; Afrikaner Nationalists oppose decision.

1915

South Africa conquers German colony of South-West Africa (Namibia).

1916

South African Native College opens at Fort Hare, Eastern Cape.

1919

Jan Smuts becomes prime minister.

1920

League of Nations grants South Africa trusteeship to govern South-West Africa.

1921

South African Communist Party formed.

1922

Government crushes rebellion by white miners ("Rand Revolt"). Industrial and Commercial Workers Union, under Clements Kadalie, becomes the first African mass movement.

1924

General Hertzog, leader of National Party, becomes prime minister in coalition with English-speaking Labor Party.

1925

Afrikaans recognized as second official language after English.

1930

White women enfranchised.

1931

All property and literacy tests removed for white voters only; Britain recognizes South Africa's legal sovereignty within the Commonwealth.

1934

Hertzog and Smuts, during worldwide depression, join forces to form the United Party under Hertzog's leadership; Afrikaner Nationalists, under Daniel Malan, break away to establish "purified" National Party.

1936

Natives Trust and Land Act, proposed in 1935, provides for eventual increase of land for African reserves from about 7 percent to 13.7 percent of all land; companion legislation removes Africans from common voters' roll in Cape Province, places them on separate roll to elect seven whites to Parliament, and creates a national advisory Natives' Representative Council; in protest, All African Convention meets in 1935 and 1936.

1939

Parliament votes 80–67 to enter World War II; South African volunteer forces, including Africans as labor auxiliaries, join Allies; Prime Minister Smuts becomes prominent Allied leader; some Afrikaner leaders advocate neutrality or support for Nazi Germany.

1943

ANC adopts charter and bill of rights calling for universal franchise; authorizes formation of Youth League, later led by Nelson Mandela and Oliver Tambo.

1946

About seventy thousand African mine workers stop work; strike broken by government forces. Natives' Representative Council adjourns indefinitely.

1948

National Party, led by Malan, wins narrow surprise victory; introduces "apartheid," which codifies and expands existing racial segregation.

1949

Legislation outlaws marriage across the color line. ANC adopts Program of Action calling for boycotts, strikes, and nonviolent civil disobedience.

1950

Population Registration Act, the "cornerstone" of apartheid, classifies all South Africans racially. Group Areas Act designates segregated residential and business areas for whites, Coloureds, and Asians. Immorality Act strengthens law prohibiting interracial sex. Suppression of Communism Act outlaws Communist Party and is used against all forms of dissent. Breadth of government repression stimulates Mandela-Tambo nationalists in the ANC to move toward multiracial alliance.

1951

Bantu Authorities Act abolishes Natives' Representative Council and establishes basis for ethnic government in African reserves, or "homelands." Bill to enable removal of Coloureds from common voters' roll by simple legislative majority provokes five-year constitutional crisis.

1952

ANC and allied groups begin nonviolent Defiance Campaign against discriminatory laws on June 26, lasting all year; about eighty-five hundred are jailed; Chief Albert Luthuli, deposed by government, is elected ANC president.

1953

Public Safety Act empowers government to declare stringent states of emergency. Bantu Education Act imposes government control over African schools and their curricula. United Party dissidents form Liberal Party, favoring nonracial but qualified franchise for blacks. Leftwing whites form Congress of Democrats in sympathy with ANC.

1955

ANC, in alliance with Indian, Coloured, and white organizations, endorses the Freedom Charter at Congress of the People; adopts it officially in 1956.

Government packs Senate and the highest court in order to remove Coloureds from common voters' roll.

1956

Coloureds placed on separate roll to elect four whites to represent them in Parliament. Twenty thousand women of all races, organized by the Federation of South African Women, march in Pretoria to protest issuance of passes to African women. Chief Luthuli, Nelson Mandela, and 154 others arrested on charges of treason; case collapses in March 1961.

1958

Dr. Hendrik Verwoerd, theoretician of apartheid, becomes prime minister.

1959

"Africanists," opposed to the role of non-Africans in the ANC and led by Robert Sobukwe, break away to form the Pan-Africanist Congress (PAC). Promotion of Bantu Self-Government Act envisages that all Africans will belong to one of eight ethnic "national units" that will eventually become independent; ends African representation by whites in Parliament. Ovamboland People's Organization is formed to oppose South African rule in South-West Africa (Namibia); becomes the South-West African People's Organization (SWAPO) in 1966. Former United Party members form Progressive Party favoring high but nonracial qualifications for the franchise; Progressive Party later becomes the Progressive Federal Party.

1960

March 21: Police kill 69 unarmed Africans and wound 186 in Sharpeville during demonstration against pass laws organized by the PAC; in unprecedented political and economic crisis following Sharpeville, government declares state of emergency (ends August 31), detains nearly two thousand activists of all races, and outlaws the ANC and PAC.

1961

Mandela and others abandon ANC's policy of nonviolence. **May 31**: South Africa leaves Commonwealth and becomes a republic. **October**: Chief Albert Luthuli awarded Nobel Peace Prize. **December**: *Umkhonto we Sizwe* ("Spear of the Nation"), armed wing of the ANC, launches sabotage campaign.

1962

Sabotage Act passed; significantly erodes rule of law. Mandela, after traveling abroad, and operating underground on his return, is arrested and sentenced to five years in prison. *Poqo* ("Africans Alone"), an offshoot of the PAC, attacks whites.

1963

"90-Day Act" virtually abrogates habeas corpus. Transkei given limited self-government. **July:** *Umkhonto* leaders arrested at Rivonia, a white Johannesburg suburb.

1964

June: Eight *Umkhonto* leaders, including Nelson Mandela, Walter Sisulu, and Govan Mbeki, sentenced to life imprisonment after admitting sabotage and preparation for guerrilla warfare (Mbeki released in 1988).

1966

September 6: Prime Minister Verwoerd assassinated; succeeded by John Vorster.

1967

Terrorism Act passed; broadened the definition of terrorism and provided for indefinite detention for those suspected of the crime.

1968

Legislation outlaws multiracial political parties. Parliamentary representation of Coloureds by whites ended. Formation of South African Students Association and Black People's Convention marks rise of black consciousness movement.

1973

January: Wave of strikes by black workers in Durban indicates growth of independent black trade union movement.

1974

April: Young officers in Lisbon, opposed to colonial wars in Africa, overthrow Portuguese government. **November:** UN General Assembly suspends credentials of South African delegation; first time UN members denied participation in General Assembly proceedings.

1975

June 25: Mozambique becomes independent. **November 11:** Angola becomes independent.

1976

June 16: Soweto students, protesting inferior education and use of Afrikaans as medium of instruction, fired on by police; countrywide protest during following months results in deaths of estimated one thousand protesters. Internal Security Act supersedes Suppression of Communism Act, broadening government's power to crush dissent. **October 26:** Transkei becomes first black South African homeland given "independence" by Pretoria (Bophuthatswana follows in 1977, Venda in 1979, and Ciskei in 1981).

1977

May 19: Winnie Mandela, wife of Nelson Mandela, banished to small farming town of Brandfort in Orange Free State. **September 12:** Steve Biko, leading exponent of black consciousness movement, dies of brain injury after police beatings while in detention. **October 19:** Government cracks down on black consciousness groups, Christian Institute, and media; detains black consciousness leaders. **November 4:** UN Security Council imposes mandatory arms embargo against South Africa.

1978

September 20: Prime Minister Vorster resigns after "Muldergate affair," a major scandal in the National Party involving misappropriation of public funds; P. W. Botha becomes prime minister. **September 29:** UN Security Council Resolution 435 endorses Western Contact Group's plan for Namibian independence.

1979

May 2: African trade unions given official recognition.

1980

April 18: Zimbabwe becomes independent. **March:** Tens of thousands of black high school and university students begin nine-month boycott of schools. **June 1:** ANC guerrillas launch new sabotage campaign by attacking three South African oil installations.

1981

Progressive Federal Party becomes official parliamentary opposition to National Party. **August 19:** Fifteen hundred squatters removed from Crossroads, a shantytown on the edge of Cape Town, and "deported" to the Transkei; most return.

1982

February: Rightwing breaks away from National Party over issue of proposed multiracial constitution and forms Conservative Party. **March:** National Forum, representing black consciousness and other government opponents, meets.

1983

August 20: United Democratic Front (UDF), a coalition of anti-apartheid organizations generally sympathetic to the Freedom Charter, launched nationally. **November:** Constitutional referendum for whites only approves racially segregated tricameral Parliament for whites, Coloureds, and Indians, but excludes Africans.

1984

March 16: Nkomati Accord, a "non-aggression and good neighborliness" pact, signed between South Africa and Mozambique. **October 16:** Anglican Bishop Desmond Tutu awarded Nobel Peace Prize for his nonviolent opposition to apartheid. **September 3:** Constitution put into effect; most widepread African uprising since Soweto erupts in the Vaal Triangle.

1985

July 21: South African government imposes state of emergency in parts of country following nearly five hundred deaths in township turmoil since September 1984. **August 15:** President Botha, in long-awaited policy address (the "Rubicon" speech), rejects foreign and domestic calls for fundamental change. **September 4:** Foreign banks suspend credit following Chase Manhattan's July 31 refusal to roll over loans; action sets off financial crisis in country. **September 9:** President Reagan imposes limited trade and financial sanctions against South Africa in move to preempt stronger measures by Congress. **November 30:** Congress of South African Trade Unions (COSATU) formed, creating largest mainly African labor federation.

1986

May: Commonwealth Eminent Persons Group (EPG) abandons attempt to mediate between South African government and its opponents after South African military attacks alleged ANC bases in neighboring states. **May-June:** After fierce fighting, pro-government "vigilantes" defeat UDF "comrades" and take control of Crossroads, a squatter settlement outside Cape Town. **June 12:** South African government imposes nationwide state of emergency. **July 1:** South African "pass laws" repealed. **October 2:** U.S. Congress overrides presidential veto and passes Comprehensive Anti-Apartheid Act (CAAA) mandating selective sanctions against South Africa. **December 11:** South African government imposes almost total censorhip on media reports of political protest.

1987

May: Conservative Party displaces Progressive Federal Party as official opposition to National Party in Parliament. **August 9:** National Union of Mineworkers (NUM) begins three-week strike—longest legal strike in South African history. **November 3:** Violence escalates around Pietermaritzburg, Natal, between supporters of Inkatha and supporters of UDF; by end of year, 230 persons killed (accord to end fighting signed in September 1988, but violence continues).

1988

February 24: South African government effectively bans seventeen anti-apartheid organizations, including the UDF; prohibits COSATU from engaging in political activities. **May 3–4:** Negotiations over Namibia's independence and removal of Cuban troops from Angola begin among Angola, Cuba, and South Africa, with United States as mediator and USSR as observer. **December 22:** Angola, Cuba, and South Africa sign two interlocking accords providing for independence of Namibia and withdrawal of 50,000 Cuban troops from Angola.

Selected Annotated Bibliography: South Africa

The books below, most of which were written for a general audience, provide an introduction to South African history, politics, and society. Most have been published in the last decade and are available in libraries and college bookstores in the United States, except for the annual surveys of the South African Institute of Race Relations. Books issued by South African publishers have been omitted, although they are an essential resource for readers who intend to study South Africa in depth.

ADAM, Heribert, and GILIOMEE, Hermann. *Ethnic Power Mobilized: Can South Africa Change?* New Haven: Yale University Press, 1979.
> A collection of essays about Afrikaner history and politics through the Vorster era.

BENSON, Mary. *Nelson Mandela: The Man and the Movement.* New York: W. W. Norton and Company, 1986.
> A sympathetic biography of the African National Congress leader imprisoned since 1962, describing his early life and political career, his nationalist beliefs, and his central role within the ANC.

BERGER, Peter L., and GODSELL, Bobby, eds. *A Future South Africa: Visions, Strategies and Realities.* Boulder, Colo.: Westview Press, 1988.
> Eight chapters by liberal analysts survey the contemporary array of political protagonists in South Africa. A conclusion by the editors predicts a slow, painful, evolutionary transition to a post-apartheid society.

BIKO, Steve. *I Write What I Like.* San Francisco: Harper & Row, 1986. (First edition: London: Bowerdean Press, 1978.)
> The collected writings of the martyred founder of the black consciousness movement, who was South Africa's most influential black leader in the post-Sharpeville era.

BRINK, André. *A Dry White Season.* New York: Morrow, 1980.
> A powerful story by South Africa's leading Afrikaner novelist about an apolitical Afrikaner teacher drawn by the death of a black friend into a web of state repression and social isolation.

BUTLER, Jeffrey; ELPHICK, Richard; and WELSH, David, eds. *Democratic Liberalism in South Africa: Its History and Prospect*. Middletown, Conn.: Wesleyan University Press, 1987.
> This book brings together twenty-four essays by white liberals who critically review the principles, policies, history, and historiography of liberalism in South Africa and argue for the continuing relevance of liberal beliefs.

COMMONWEALTH GROUP OF EMINENT PERSONS. *Mission to South Africa: The Commonwealth Report*. New York: Viking Penguin, 1986.
> The findings of a special Commonwealth delegation that conferred widely with all sides in the South African conflict in early 1986 in an unsuccessful attempt to initiate a dialogue. The report is a highly readable analysis of the problems of political change.

CRAPANZANO, Vincent. *Waiting: The Whites of South Africa*. New York: Vintage Books, 1986.
> An American anthropologist's portrait of a small community in the western Cape where whites are involved in a religious revival with apocalyptic dimensions. Explores the effects of domination on those who dominate.

DAVIS, Stephen M. *Apartheid's Rebels: Inside South Africa's Hidden War*. New Haven: Yale University Press, 1987.
> Focusing on the African National Congress in its exile years, this book offers the fullest portrait to date of the ANC's guerrilla campaign.

DENOON, Donald, and NYEKO, Balam. *Southern Africa Since 1800,* new edition. New York: Longman, 1984.
> Traces the political and economic evolution of the region through modern times and draws on new interpretive themes in the South African historiography of the 1970s.

DUGARD, John. *Human Rights and the South African Legal Order*. Princeton: Princeton University Press, 1978.
> An introduction to what the author, a prominent South African jurist, calls "the pursuit of justice within an unjust legal order." Covers the laws involving civil rights and liberties, state security laws, judicial procedures in political trials, and the South African judiciary.

FINNEGAN, William. *Crossing the Line: A Year in the Land of Apartheid*. New York: Harper & Row, 1986.
> An appealing memoir by a young American writer who discovers South Africa through teaching at a Coloured high school in Cape Town.

FREDERIKSE, Julie. *A Different Kind of War: From Soweto to Pretoria*. Boston: Beacon Press, 1987.
> A political portrait of the years between the Soweto uprising of 1976 and the state of emergency imposed in the mid-1980s. The author

uses passages from interviews, trial statements, news articles, and political ephemera, together with photographs and graphics, to capture the emotionally charged atmosphere of this decade.

FREDRICKSON, George M. *White Supremacy: A Comparative Study in American and South African History.* New York: Oxford University Press, 1981.
An interpretive work by an American historian on the causes, character, and consequences of white supremacist ideology and practice.

GELDENHUYS, Deon. *The Diplomacy of Isolation: South African Foreign Policy Making.* New York: St. Martin's Press, 1984.
An authoritative look at the foreign policymaking process under Vorster and Botha, elaborated with a wealth of illustrative detail.

GERHART, Gail M. *Black Power in South Africa: The Evolution of an Ideology.* Berkeley: University of California Press, 1978.
Explores the historical strain of African nationalism, still popular today, which eschews white participation in black liberation movements.

GOODWIN, June. *Cry Amandla! South African Women and the Question of Power.* New York: Africana Publishing Co., 1984.
A portrayal of the contrasting perspectives of white and African women on issues of power and privilege, by a former correspondent of the *Christian Science Monitor.*

GORDIMER, Nadine. *Burger's Daughter.* New York: Viking Press, 1979.
This, the most political of Gordimer's novels, is loosely based on the life and legacy of Abram Fischer, a distinguished Afrikaner lawyer sentenced to life imprisonment for his role in South Africa's underground Communist Party.

GRUNDY, Kenneth W. *The Militarization of South African Politics.* Bloomington: Indiana University Press, 1986.
An examination of the increasing influence of the military establishment in fashioning both foreign and domestic security policy for the South African government.

HANLON, Joseph. *Beggar Your Neighbours: Apartheid Power in South Africa.* Bloomington: Indiana University Press, 1986.
A comprehensive assessment of political, military, and economic relationships between South Africa and the Front Line States by a journalist critical of South Africa's policies.

HANLON, Joseph, and OMOND, Roger. *The Sanctions Handbook.* New York: Viking Penguin, 1987.
A summary of the evidence, the arguments, and the politics surrounding the sanctions debate in the United States and Britain.

HARRISON, David. *The White Tribe of Africa: South Africa in Perspective.* Berkeley and Los Angeles: University of California Press, 1981.
Engaging and informative sketches of personalities and episodes in Afrikaner history.

JOUBERT, Elsa. *Poppie*. London: Hodder and Stoughton, 1980.
A novel that movingly portrays the needless human suffering caused by the apartheid system and the forbearance of its victims.

KANE-BERMAN, John. *South Africa: A Method in the Madness*. London: Pluto Press, 1979. [Published in South Africa under the title: *Soweto—Black Revolt, White Reaction*. Johannesburg: Ravan Press, 1978.]
An informative account of the causes and circumstances surrounding the Soweto revolt of 1976–77, written by a journalist who later became director of the South African Institute of Race Relations.

KARIS, Thomas, and CARTER, Gwendolen, eds. *From Protest to Challenge: A Documentary History of African Politics in South Africa 1882–1964* (four volumes). Stanford: Hoover Institution Press, 1972–77.
A comprehensive survey of the history of extraparliamentary black and allied opposition groups. Volumes 1–3 contain primary source documents explained in their historical context, and Volume 4 presents biographical profiles of over three hundred political leaders.

LELYVELD, Joseph. *Move Your Shadow: South Africa, Black and White*. New York: Times Books, 1985.
A Pulitzer Prize-winning book by a *New York Times* correspondent. Sensitively chronicles the tragedy and absurdity of apartheid.

LIPTON, Merle. *Capitalism and Apartheid: South Africa, 1910–1984*. Totowa, N.J.: Rowman and Allanheld, 1985.
A lucid contribution to the debate about the historic and possible future role of capitalism in fostering racial inequality. The author, a South African-born economist, comes down on the side of nonracial capitalism.

LODGE, Tom. *Black Politics in South Africa Since 1945*. New York: Longman, 1983.
A well-documented interpretation of key events, issues, and personalities in the African nationalist struggle, by a leading authority on the subject.

MACSHANE, Denis; Plaut, Martin; and Ward, David. *Power! Black Workers, Their Unions and the Struggle for Freedom in South Africa*. Boston: South End Press, 1984.
An introduction to the South African trade union movement; less authoritative than Steven Friedman's *Building Tomorrow Today: African Workers in Trade Unions 1970–1984,* published in South Africa by the Ravan Press in 1987.

MATHABANE, Mark. *Kaffir Boy: The True Story of a Black Youth's Coming of Age in Apartheid South Africa*. New York: Macmillan, 1986.
An autobiographical account of life in Alexandra, long one of South Africa's poorest and most neglected black townships. The author describes his struggle to obtain an education and to escape the straitjacket of apartheid.

MERMELSTEIN, David, ed. *The Anti-Apartheid Reader: South Africa and the Struggle Against White Racist Rule*. New York: Grove Press, 1987.
   A wide-ranging anthology of eighty pieces excerpted from the writings of scholars, journalists, and activists. Provides a thought-provoking excursion through the complexities of the current South African scene.

MINTER, William. *King Solomon's Mines Revisited: Western Interests and the Burdened History of South Africa*. New York: Basic Books, 1986.
   One of America's leading anti-apartheid activists reviews the history of U.S. and British involvement in the economic exploitation of southern Africa and makes the case for sanctions.

MUTLOATSE, Mothobi, ed. *Africa South: Contemporary Writings*. Exeter, N.H.: Heinemann Educational Books, 1981.
   An anthology of short stories and other pieces by South Africa's current generation of black writers.

OMOND, Roger. *The Apartheid Handbook: A Guide to South Africa's Everyday Racial Policies*. New York: Viking Penguin, 1985.
   Arranged in simple question-and-answer form, this is a detailed factual guide to the racial laws and practices of South Africa in the mid-1980s.

SAMPSON, Anthony. *Black and Gold: Tycoons, Revolutionaries and Apartheid*. New York: Pantheon Books, 1987.
   A highly readable analysis of the relationship between international business and black nationalism in the modern era, by a British writer and journalist with long South African experience.

SAUL, John, and GELB, Stephen. *The Crisis in South Africa,* revised edition. New York: Monthly Review Press, 1986.
   An influential Marxist analysis of what the authors perceive as an "organic crisis" in the South African system that will lead to its ultimate demise.

SECRETARY OF STATE'S ADVISORY COMMITTEE ON SOUTH AFRICA. *A U.S. Policy Toward South Africa*. Washington, D.C.: U.S. Department of State, January 1987.
   A post-U.S. sanctions assessment of the situation in South Africa and an incisive critique of the Reagan administration's policy of constructive engagement.

SMITH, David M., ed. *Living Under Apartheid: Aspects of Urbanization and Social Change in South Africa*. Boston: George Allen & Unwin, 1982.
   A collection of twelve essays on housing, land use, migration, unemployment, and other contemporary social issues.

SOUTH AFRICAN INSTITUTE OF RACE RELATIONS. *Race Relations Survey*. Johannesburg. Annual publication.
   This yearly compendium of facts, events, and statistics, published in South Africa, is an invaluable resource for research on social and political developments.

STUDY COMMISSION ON U.S. POLICY TOWARD SOUTHERN AFRICA. *South Africa: Time Running Out*. Berkeley: University of California Press and Foreign Policy Study Foundation, 1981.
  One of the most comprehensive introductions to South Africa and to U.S. interests and policy options; a useful reference work.

THOMPSON, Leonard. *A History of South Africa*. New Haven: Yale University Press, 1990.
  Covers South African history from precolonial times to the present; written for the general reader but synthesizes the best of modern scholarship.

VILLA-VICENCIO, Charles, and DE GRUCHY, John W., eds. *Resistance and Hope: South African Essays in Honour of Beyers Naudé*. Grand Rapids: Wm. B. Eerdmans Publishing Co., 1985.
  Tutu, Boesak, Chikane, Tlhagale, and other prominent church leaders have contributed chapters to this collection of essays on religion in contemporary South Africa.

WILSON, Francis, and RAMPHELE, Mamphela. *Uprooting Poverty: The South African Challenge. Report for the Second Carnegie Inquiry into Poverty and Development in Southern Africa*. New York: W. W. Norton and Company, 1989.
  A vivid and extensively documented landmark study of socioeconomic conditions affecting South Africa's impoverished majority. The authors draw on the work of dozens of researchers in the fields of health, employment, literacy, and housing and present recommendations for transforming South African society.

This bibliography was prepared by Gail Gerhart, Ph.D., currently on the faculty of the Department of Political Science, Columbia University.

APPENDICES

APPENDIX A

TransAfrica News Report, Special Edition, August 1981

The following documents were leaked to TransAfrica, the black American lobby group for Africa and the Caribbean, and published as a special edition of the TransAfrica News Report *in August 1981. There were six documents in all, four prepared by U.S. State Department officials and two by the South African government:*

1. *Memorandum of Conversation between Assistant Secretary of State Chester Crocker and South African Foreign Minister Pik Botha and Defense Minister Magnus Malan, Pretoria, April 15–16, 1981.*
2. *State Department overview of U.S. policy toward southern Africa, May 31, 1981.*
3. *Memorandum from Paul J. Hare, director of State Department's Southern African Affairs office, to Chester Crocker on Contact Group meeting of May 13, 1981.*
4. *Crocker's "Scope Paper" for Secretary of State Alexander Haig in preparation for Haig's meeting with Pik Botha on May 14, 1981.*
5. *South Africa's list of U.S. interests in southern Africa, May 1981.*
6. *South African memorandum on U.S.–South African nuclear relations, May 14, 1981.*

These documents are reproduced from the special edition of TransAfrica News Report. *Together they provide a fascinating insight into the early stages of the Reagan administration's dealings with the South African government. As the only primary source material currently available, they also reveal the evolution of Chester Crocker's thinking and the response of the South Africans as constructive engagement got under way.*

1) MEMORANDUM OF PRETORIA MEETING

Memorandum of Conversation

Participants:	*South Africa:*
	Foreign Minister Pik Botha
	Defense Minister Magnus Malan
	U.S.:
	Assistant Secretary-designate Crocker
	Alan Keyes, S/P
Date & Place:	April 15/16, 1981, Pretoria
Subject:	Discussions with SAG
Copies to:	AF, IO-McElhaney, S/P-Keyes, AF/S

U.S.-Africa Relations:

Botha opened first day's discussion by expressing unhappiness over
what SAG perceives as backsliding by Administration from view of
South Africa taken during U.S. presidential campaign. Reagan campaign statements produced high expectations in South Africa. But,
administration, in response to views of allies, such as UK and Germany, and to influence State Department professionals, has disappointed SAG expectations. USG handling of visit by military officers
example of this. Botha raised issue of trust, referring to earlier
"McHenry" duplicity on issue of SWAPO bases.

   However, he affirmed that it means a great deal to SAG to have
good relations with U.S. and that SAG understands U.S. problems in
maintaining friendly relations with black African states. To begin
second day's discussion, Crocker noted that, though he hadn't come
to discuss South Africa's internal affairs, it was clear that positive
movement domestically would make it easier for the U.S. to work
with SAG. U.S. ability to develop full relations with SAG depends on
success of Prime Minister Botha's program and extent to which it is
seen as broadening SAG's domestic support. "Pik" Botha cautioned
against making success of P.W. Botha's program a condition of
U.S./African relations. Crocker responded with view that this is not a
condition but reflects U.S desire to support positive trends. In response Pik Botha went more fully into reasons for deep SAG distrust
of U.S. Botha reiterated view that, as result of pressure from African
states in UN, and influence of State Department, USG has backed
away from initial recognition of importance of its interests in southern Africa (read South Africa). He doubted whether, given domestic
pressures and views of such African states as Nigeria, U.S. could

continue any policy favorable to South Africa, which would not provoke constant criticism.

In response, Crocker replied that present Administration would have more backbone in face of pressure than previous one. U.S. has many diverse interests and responsibilities, but will stand up for what we think right. Our objective is to increase SAG confidence.

Toward end of discussion, in context of Angola issue, Botha again came back to question of trust. He said he is suspicious of U.S. because of way U.S. dropped SAG in Angola in 1975. He argued that SAG went into Angola with USG support, then U.S. voted to condemn in UN. Cited many examples of past USG decisions that didn't inspire confidence—Vietnam, Iran, USG failure to support moderate governments in Africa, while aiding those with leftist rhetoric. Alluding to Chad, Botha asserted that African leaders became so desperate for help against Qadafi that one even approached SAG privately, as last resort, to ask for help. Botha admitted that SAG can't yet pass judgment on present Administration. He pleaded for consistency, "When we say something, let's stick to it."

Crocker addressed trust issue, saying that new Administration is tired of double think and double talk. Despite rocky start in U.S./SAG relations, improvement is possible. Reagan election victory represents enormous change in U.S. public opinion on foreign policy reversing trend of post-Vietnam years.

SAG View of Regional Situation

During first day's session Botha discussed at length situation in southern Africa and Africa at large. He cited economic, food and population problems to support view that Africa is a dying continent because Africans have made a mess of their independence. Botha asserted belief that cause isn't race, but fact that new nations lack experience, cultural background, technical training.

Referring to South African past experience in helping and training blacks in neighboring states, Botha discussed the need for peaceful co-existence between South Africa and its neighbors. Until they recognize they're making a mess of their independence, South Africa can't help them. South Africa is willing to help those who admit they need its help.

On this basis Botha presented vision of southern Africa's future, in context of "Constellation of States" concept. He appealed for USG support for South Africa's view of region's future, involving a confederation of states, each independent, but linked by a centralizing secretariat. SAG doesn't expect U.S. support for apartheid, but it hopes there will be no repeat of Mondale's "One Man, One Vote" statement. SAG goal is survival of white values, not white privileges.

Botha argued that central issue in southern Africa is subversion. Noting that what ANC does, South Africa can do better, Botha stressed need for agreement on non-use of force. If regions starts to collapse, fire will spread, there will be no winners. This is not meant as threat, but simply stating facts. Botha emphasized view that if you kill the part of Africa containing people who can do things, you kill whole of Africa.

Asked about U.S view of the importance of southern Africa, Crocker summarized U.S. regional interests in context of its global responsibilities. He emphasized U.S. desire to deal with destabilization threats worldwide by going to their sources, using means tailored to each source and region involved. Crocker made clear that in Africa we distinguish between countries where Soviets and Cubans have a combat presence, and those whose governments espousing Marxism for their own practical purposes. He stressed that top U.S. priority is to stop Soviet encroachment in Africa. U.S. wants to work with SAG, but ability to deal with Soviet presence severely impeded by Namibia. Crocker alluded to black African view that South Africa contributes to instability in region. Said he agrees with this view to extent SAG goes beyond reprisal. Putting fear in minds of inferior powers makes them irrational.

Namibia/Angola Issue

Malan raised topic of Angola during first session. He asked about a supposed U.S. plan for an all-African force to replace the Cubans in Angola. Crocker responded that he was aware of no such plan, except perhaps as a symbolic gesture. Views were exchanged on the character of the MPLA Government, with the South Africans firmly asserting its domination by Moscow, while Crocker suggested a more nuanced view, allowing for several factions within the MPLA varying in ideological commitment and character. Discussion touched briefly on the nature of SWAPO. Botha alluded to the view that Nujoma is a "Bloody Thug."

Malan flatly declared that the SAG can't accept prospects of a SWAPO victory which brings Soviet/Cuban forces to Walvis Bay. This would result from any election which left SWAPO in a dominant position. Therefore a SWAPO victory would be unacceptable in the context of a Westminster-type political system. Namibia needs a federal system. SAG does not rule out an internationally acceptable settlement, but could not live with a SWAPO victory that left SWAPO unchecked power. Botha asserted that Ovambo dominance after the election would lead to civil war.

Crocker addressed these concerns saying USG recognized need to build South African confidence and security. Malan interposed with the view that it is the local people in Namibia who need security, and SAG could accept SWAPO victory only if their security is provided for. SAG can't dictate to local parties. Crocker remarked upon need to negotiate with governments, which ultimately means that parties can't have veto power. In response Botha gave eloquent rendition of SAG's problem in dealing with the internal parties. These parties fear secret plot to install SWAPO government. SAG doesn't wish to entrench white privileges but some confidence-building measures needed. Discussion briefly explored constitutional issues. South Africans asked who would write a constitution. Crocker alluded to idea of expert panel.

SAG sees Savimbi in Angola as buffer for Namibia. SAG believes Savimbi wants southern Angola. Having supported him this far, it would damage SAG honor if Savimbi is harmed.

Second round of discussions went into greater detail on Namibia/Angola questions. Malan declared SAG view that Angola/Namibia situation is number one problem in southern Africa. Angola is one place where U.S. can roll back Soviet/Cuban presence in Africa. Need to get rid of Cubans, and support UNITA. UNITA is going from strength to strength, while SWAPO grows militarily weaker.

In his response Crocker agreed on relation of Angola to Namibia. USG believes it would be possible to improve U.S./South African relations if Namibia were no longer an issue. We seek a settlement, but one in our interest, based on democratic principles. Our view is that South Africa is under no early military pressure to leave Namibia. The decision belongs to SAG, and ways must be found to address its concerns. USG assumes Soviet/Cuban presence is one of those concerns, and we are exploring ways to remove it in context of Namibia settlement. We agree that UNITA is an important factor in the Angolan situation. We believe there can be no peace in Angola without reconciliation between UNITA and MPLA. We see no prospect of military victory for UNITA. Must achieve movement toward reconciliation by playing on divisions in MPLA. With regard to Namibia, USG assumes that constitution is an important issue, which must be resolved before elections. The constitution would include guarantees for minority rights and democratic processes. We have said we believe SCR 435 is a basis for transition to independence for Namibia, but not for a full settlement. We wish to meet SAG concerns, while taking account of views on other side. We cannot scrap 435 without great difficulty. We wish to supplement rather than discard it.

Malan took up Namibian question, observing that internationalization of the issue posed greatest difficulty. He alluded to tremendous distrust of UN in South Africa. He questioned inclusion of South Africa and Front Line states in the quest for a settlement, asserting that SWAPO and the internal parties should conclude it. He agreed on the need for a constitution. But 435 can't work. The longer it takes to solve the Namibia question, the less South African presence will be required there. We will reach a stage where internal forces in Namibia can militarily defeat SWAPO.

Malan's remarks set stage for Botha to discuss SAG view of SWAPO. Botha noted that SAG thought it was important to U.S. to stop Soviet gains. But if you say SWAPO not Marxist, you move in same direction as previous administration. SWAPO's people are indoctrinated in Marxism every day. Savimbi considers SWAPO universally Marxist. SAG's bottom line is no Moscow flag in Windhoek. If U.S. disagrees, let sanctions go on, and get out of the situation. South Africa can survive sanctions. Eventually South Africa can get support of moderate black African states. Better to start U.S./SAG relations with lower expectations, than to disagree angrily later. At moment, U.S. doesn't believe SAG view of SWAPO; you're soft on SWAPO. SAG appreciates U.S. firmness against Soviets, Botha continued. Even Africans now see you assuming leadership. But SAG worried that USG is moving toward Namibia plan SAG cannot understand. As with Kissinger attempt on Rhodesia, it will be difficult to get consensus, especially with so many parties involved. SAG tried one-on-one approach with Angolans, but Geneva meetings sidetracked effort. SAG has tried Angolans several times. Each time there is progress, but then something intervenes. We're convinced SWAPO is Marxist. Nujoma will nationalize the whole place, and cause upheaval and civil war, involving countries as well. We are pleading for you to see the dangers of a wrong solution in Namibia. It would be better to have a low-level conflict there indefinitely, than to have a civil war escalating to a general conflagration. If Nujoma governs as an Ovambo, the Hereros will fight. Also, Nujoma made promises to the Soviets. Defectors from SWAPO have revealed their plan to SAG—first Namibia, then Botswana, Lesotho, and Swaziland, followed by the final attack on South Africa. SAG can't ignore this reality. We wouldn't justify that to our people. South Africa is a democracy as far as white voters are concerned. Even black leaders can criticize the government. South Africa has freedom, and can have more, but survival is the prerequisite. The BLS leaders agree with us. Even some Front Line leaders see the danger. We have twice saved Kaunda's life.

The situation is not what you think. You think in global terms; we're not a global power. We must safeguard our interests here. Not just white interests. We see the necessity of avoiding black-white polarization. But we see it as an ideological struggle. Developed moderate blacks are not communists. They will engage with us in common effort against communism. When whites see blacks as allies, whites will move away from discrimination. With more distribution of economic goods, more blacks will join us. But if we all come under Moscow's domination, that's the end.

Crocker addressed Botha's expressed fears and concerns by first accepting the premise that Soviet domination is the danger. But U.S. believes best way to avoid that danger is to get Namibia issue behind us. As long as issue subsists, we cannot reach a situation where U.S. can engage with South Africa in security, and include South Africa in our general security framework. If Namibia continues, it will open South/Central Africa to the Soviets. Simmering conflict in Namibia is not acceptable. The ideas U.S. has in mind don't include Soviets in Windhoek. We believe we can get the Soviets out of Angola, and provide a guarantee of security whether Nujoma wins or not.

Botha said this is the nitty-gritty. Without Soviet support, others won't accept Nujoma's rule. To satisfy others we need a political solution. Crocker agreed that a political solution is needed. Botha stressed the need to consult with leaders in Namibia. If U.S. can gain their confidence, and SWAPO's, and talk about minority rights, progress is possible. People in Namibia are concerned about property, an independent judiciary, freedom of religion, the preservation of their language and the quality of education under the present system, discrimination has been abolished by law, though it continues in practice. There is also the problem of the white ethnic Legislature vs. the black majority Council of Ministers

Crocker said that U.S. understands concern with constitutional rights. U.S. has inherited a situation with many parties but we must build a consensus in Africa that we are serious and not just delaying. We believe a Lancaster type conference won't work. We see a panel of experts, consulting all parties, writing a constitution, and then selling it through the Contact Group. With SAG's help, we could sell it to the internal parties. Botha referred to reports of a French constitutional plan. He said that he's against multiple plans. Botha stressed need for U.S. leadership, and emphasized need for U.S. to consult with internal parties in Namibia. He discussed SAG relations with internal leaders, and need to avoid leaving them in lurch in order not to be discredited with other moderate leaders in Africa. He tied this to possibility of SAG cooperating with moderate African states to deal with economic development problems. Botha concluded by saying that SAG doesn't want to let Namibia go the wrong way; that's why South Africa is willing to pay the price of the war. We pray and hope for a government favorably disposed to us. The internal parties don't want us to let go until they have sufficient power to control the situation. We want an anti-Soviet black government.

Following the substantive discussion, Botha conveyed to Crocker written communications from the heads of Bophuthatswana and Venda. He explained that their ambassadors wanted to deliver the messages in person, but Botha decided to convey them to avoid appearance of trying to force U.S. hand. Then question of invitation to Botha to visit U.S. in May was discussed. Crocker stressed need for SAG to decide cooperation with U.S. was worth it before accepting invitation. Botha resisted setting any conditions for visit, and said he would prefer not to come if conditions are set. Crocker said there were no conditions, just a question of clarifying the spirit in which the visit would take place. Botha ended the discussion by noting that he would inform internal parties about discussion immediately. He said he would tell Prime Minister Botha that SAG should explore question of constitution before an election in Namibia. He noted that a referendum on the constitution, rather than constituent assembly elections, would make matters easier.

2) STATE DEPARTMENT SUMMARY/OVERVIEW OF CROCKER TRIP

Southern Africa
Drafted: AF/S:RCFrasure:mo
5/31/81 x28252
Cleared:IO/UNP:DMcElhaney
Approved:AF/S:PJHare

Essential Factors

In the second phase of our review of southern Africa policy, Assistant Secretary-designate Crocker traveled April 6-23 to twelve African countries to discuss our initial thoughts on how we might proceed on Namibia and other issues and to hear the views of interested governments. On Namibia, Crocker found the Front Line states and Nigeria rhetorically unyielding in their insistence that the only acceptable solution to the problem was the immediate implementation of an unchanged UNSCR 435, to be brought about by Western pressure on South Africa. Crocker responded that in our view possible changes and add-ons to 435 including constitutional arrangements would have to be considered if we wished to solve the Namibia problem. The South Africans were equally firm in their discussions with us. Although they were willing to accept the UN as an umbrella for a Namibia settlement, they are extremely reluctant to move forward to any solution that would entail a SWAPO government in Windhoek. The issue of Namibia will be a central theme in Secretary Haig's meeting with Pik Botha in Washington on May 14.

The Assistant Secretary-designate's trip concluded with a Contract Group meeting in London on April 22-23. At that meeting, the Five were substantially in agreement that we should develop new proposals in several areas in an effort to get the settlement process moving. That consensus was confirmed by foreign ministers at the May 3 Contact Group meeting in Rome. At the conclusion of that meeting, the Five in a communique:

- "Reaffirmed their conviction that only a settlement under the aegis of the United Nations would be acceptable to the international community."
- "Stated their belief that Security Council Resolution 435 provides a solid basis for the achievement of a negotiated settlement."

- "Decided to develop proposals encompassing measures, including constitutional arrangements, with the aim of enhancing prospects of achieving a negotiated settlement."

Senior officials of the Five at the Crocker level will meet in Washington in late May to begin the development of these new proposals.

The EC position on southern Africa is a reflection of the national positions of the FRG, France and the UK in the Contact Group.

Suggested Points

- The USG in concert with our Contact Group colleagues remains committed to an internationally acceptable settlement in Namibia.
- Our views were reflected in the May 3 Rome communique.

3) HARE MEMORANDUM TO CROCKER

May 13, 1981

TO:　　AF – Chester A. Crocker
FROM:　AF/S – Paul J. Hare
SUBJECT: Your Meeting with the Secretary Wednesday, May 13, 4:00 P.M.

You may wish to add to your checklist a brief account of the May 12 Contact Group meeting. Everyone seemed to agree that in the Pik Botha visit we should be aiming at getting a better understanding of whether South Africa would be willing to move forward toward a restructured, internationally acceptable settlement. In particular, however, our interlocutors are:
- very leery of holding out the prospect to the SAG that we are willing to change UNSCR 435. They feel that will induce South African creativity, in particular a reinvigorated SAG assault on UNTAG which they see as the

guts of 435. Part of the problem is semantical, i.e., they assent we should describe our efforts as attempts to "complement" rather than to "change" 435.

- generally reluctant to get involved in a fullblown constitution. The Canadians (at least Paul La Pointe) are in the lead on this issue claiming that a set of principles is sufficient. La Pointe's argument lacks logic and merit.

- in agreement that guarantees will need to be explored. Nevertheless, we are all certain that this is an especially delicate issue in which too much clarity on points such as Walvis Bay and enforceability are not desirable and should certainly not be discussed with the South Africans at this stage of the process.

Drafted: AF/S:RCFrasure:mo

4) CROCKER'S "SCOPE PAPER" FOR HAIG

TO: The Secretary
FROM: AF – Chester A. Crocker
SUBJECT: Your Meeting with South African Foreign Minister Botha, 11:00 a.m., May 14, at the Department—Scope Paper

Summary:

The political relationship between the United States and South Africa has now arrived at a crossroads of perhaps historic significance. After twenty years of generally increasing official U.S. Government coolness toward South Africa and concomitant South African intransigence, the possibility may exist for a more positive and reciprocal relationship between the two countries based upon shared strategic concerns in southern Africa, our recognition that the government of P. W. Botha represents a unique opportunity for domestic change, and willingness of the Reagan Administration to deal realistically with South Africa. The problem of Namibia, however, which complicates our relations with our European allies and with black Africa, is a primary obstacle to the development of a new relationship with South Africa. It also represents an opportunity to counter the Soviet threat in Africa. We thus need Pretoria's cooperation in working toward an internationally acceptable solution to

Namibia which would, however, safeguard U.S. and South African essential interests and concerns.

I. Objectives:

- To tell the South Africans that we are willing with them to open a new chapter in our relationship based upon strategic reality and South Africa's position in that reality and the continued explicit commitment of P.W. Botha's government to domestic change.
- To make clear to the South Africans that we see the continuation of the Namibia problem as a primary obstacle to the development of that new relationship and that we are willing to work with them toward an internationally acceptable settlement which will not harm their interests.

II. Participants:

U.S.	South Africa
The Secretary	Foreign Minister Botha
Under Secretary Stoessel	Brand Fourie
Assistant Secretary-	Ambassador Sole
Designate Crocker	Ambassador Ecksteen
Assistant Secretary Abrams	

III. Setting:

The discussions with the South Africans will cover three discrete areas: Namibia, U.S.–South Africa nuclear cooperation and general bilateral issues. Pik Botha may touch on each of these during his 15 minutes in private with you. Botha will probably weave these questions into an overview of southern Africa regional issues delivered in terms of his familiar "Africa is dying"/Soviet-onslaught-against South Africa" speech. The expanded meeting with you and the working luncheon will focus specifically on Namibia. OES Assistant Secretary Jim Malone will conduct separate discussions with Brand Fourie on the nuclear issue. I will also conduct a separate discussion with Fourie on our bilateral relations with reference to the several specific issues now pending between us. This format will permit you to focus on the Namibia issue.

Our dialogue with South Africa over the possibility of a new and more balanced relationship began with my visit to Pretoria last month. As I reported to you from my meetings with Pik Botha and Defense Minister Magnus Malan, I found the South Africans to be in a testy mood. The substantial amounts of misinformation and disinformation which had appeared in the press since the November election had, I suspect, acted to bring to the surface ingrained distrust. The South Africans are deeply suspicious of us, of our will, from the 1975-76 experience and the Carter period. They claim that they can go it alone in the region—an attitude which is partly bluster, partly an opening bargaining position with us.

South African truculence (which can be coated with great charm) is compounded by the fact that, as an international pariah, the country has "had no meaningful, balanced bilateral relations in recent memory." Thus, the South Africans deeply resent being treated as an embarrassment and are not used to the give-and-take of pragmatic relations. If the South Africans still want to vent their frustrations, I fear you will be subjected to Pik's rhetoric. Thus, it is in your interest to take control of the meeting from the beginning.

IV. Discussion of Objectives:

1. To tell the South Africans that we are willing with them to open a new chapter in our relationship based upon strategic reality and South Africa's position in that reality and the continued explicit commitment of P. W. Botha's government to domestic change.

You will need to make it clear to Pik that we share the South African hope that, despite political differences among the states of southern Africa, the economic interdependence of the area and constructive internal change within South Africa can be the foundations for a new era of cooperation, stability, and security in the region. We also share their view that the chief threat to the realization of this hope is the presence and influence in the region of the Soviet Union and its allies.

You will also need to make it clear to Pik that we are not willing to be manipulated by them or to act as a smokescreen for their actions and misadventures with their neighbors. We must make it clear to the South Africans that we have a role in rebuilding stability in southern Africa, that is a shared goal they cannot reach without us, and they cannot go it alone. Our shared objectives require that our diplomacy have a chance to operate and our interests be observed as well as theirs. We cannot afford to give them a blank check regionally. Moreover, SAG intransigence and violent adventures will expand Soviet opportunities and reduce Western leverage in Africa. In turn, they may complain about our performance in the past and voice doubts about our constancy and reliability in the future.

Talking Points

- We want to open a new chapter in relations with South Africa.
- We feel the new relationship should be based upon our shared hopes for the future prosperity, security and stability of southern Africa, constructive internal change within South Africa and our shared perception of the role of the Soviet Union and its surrogates in thwarting those goals.
- We can foresee cooperating with you in a number of ways in our efforts to reestablish regional stability.
- U.S./South African cooperation is indispensable for the success of those efforts. Failure to cooperate will encourage further Soviet gains, and jeopardize the interests of both our countries.
- We will not allow others to dictate what our relationship with South Africa will be as evidenced by our recent veto of sanctions. But just as we recognize your permanent stake in the future of southern Africa, so you must recognize our permanent interest in Africa as a whole.
- We must consider these interests in our southern African policy and expect you will take them into account in your dealings with us. This will require restraint and good will by all parties. We cannot consent to act as a smokescreen for actions which excite the fears of other states in the region, and encourage impractical, emotional responses to regional problems.
- Although we may continue to differ on apartheid, and cannot condone a system of institutionalized racial differentiation, we can cooperate with a society undergoing constructive change. Your government's explicit commitment in this direction will enable us to work with you. You must help to make this approach credible. You also should recognize that this period represents

your best shot, a rare opportunity, because of our mandate and our desire to turn a new leaf in bilateral relations.

- The new situation we envision in southern Africa would entail mutual recognition of the principles of inviolability of borders and non-interference in internal affairs in the states of the region.
- Our cooperative relationship would also recognize the key economic role played by South Africa in the region and the major contributions which could be made by South Africa to coordinated regional economic development.
- I understand that in a separate meeting here you will be discussing practical steps we can undertake to begin the process of improving our bilateral relations.

2. To make clear to the South Africans that we see U.S./SAG cooperation in resolving the Namibian problem as the crucial first phase of our new relationship and that we are willing to work with them toward an internationally acceptable settlement which will safeguard their interests and reflect our mutual desire to foreclose Soviet gains in southern Africa.

Namibia complicates our relations with our European allies and with black Africa, and the interests of South Africa with those states as well. We cannot allow the South Africans to be disingenuous with us over Namibia. If they have no intention of pulling out of the territory under circumstances reasonably acceptable to the international community at large, we will want to opt out of the negotiation process rather than be subjected to the endless, meaningless charade. Contrary to what Botha will argue, UN involvement will be necessary to gain international acceptance for a Namibia settlement. As he told Crocker in Pretoria, there is no point in fooling around, dissimulation or miscommunication.

Conversely, if the South Africans cooperate: to achieve an internationally acceptable settlement, this will greatly facilitate efforts to deal effectively with the Soviet threat. We need to convey our seriousness about this strategic choice. A relationship initiated on a cooperative basis could move forward toward a future in which South Africa returns to a place within the regional framework of Western security interests. The South Africans will be anxious to explore the details of such future relationship. We cannot be excessive in what we suggest to them, e.g., any implication that we can return to 1945 is unrealistic given firm international commitments such as the arms embargo. We can, however, work to end South Africa's polecat status in the world and seek to restore its place as a legitimate and important regional actor with whom we can cooperate pragmatically. You will also need to respond with an artful combination of gestures and hints. The gestures would include, as described in the attached paper, small but concrete steps such as the normalization of our military attaché relationship.

Talking Points

- The continuation of Namibia as a festering problem complicates our relations with our European allies and bedevils our relations with Black Africa. It complicates your relations with those countries as well and prevents South Africa from improving its relations with its neighbors.

  As you told Crocker in Pretoria, there is no point in dissimulation or miscommunication between us.
- We share your view that Namibia not be turned over to the Soviets and their allies. A Russian flag in Windhoek is as unacceptable to us as it is to you.
- We believe that a carefully conceived and implemented Namibia settlement will help to foreclose opportunities for growth of Soviet influence in southern Africa, and can, in the course of such a settlement, contribute to the leverage we need to produce a withdrawal of Soviet/Cuban military forces from Angola.
- We seek your sincere cooperation in developing conclusive criteria for a settlement which leads to a truly independent Namibia, while enhancing our efforts against Soviet encroachment and safeguarding the interests of U.S., South Africa and all the people of Namibia.
- This approach can facilitate a deepening of our bilateral relations in mutually beneficial ways. It can also begin a process leading to the end of international rejection of your country and greater acceptance of South Africa within the global framework of Western security.
- We did not invite you here to sell you specifics of a Namibia plan. Rather we want to explore the depth and seriousness of your interest in a settlement.
- We are inevitably brokers in this exercise. You must tell us two things (A) whether you are in fact prepared to

move to a settlement now, to commit yourselves to implement a revised plan once we pin down specifics; (B)
what your conclusive list of concerns includes. We will
make our best efforts to meet your concerns but you
must respect our role as broker and the crucial importance of African acceptance.
- My people need to begin shaping revised proposals. Our
credibility is on the line. We need to know SAG's authoritative position.

5) SOUTH AFRICAN LISTING OF U.S. INTERESTS IN RELATIONS WITH SOUTH AFRICA

1. Security of access to critical minerals.
2. Safeguarding the Cape sea route including the capacity to prevent the Soviet Union from interfering with
   shipping in the Mozambique channel and around the
   Cape.
3. The protection of American financial and trade interests in the southern African region.
4. Removal of military forces of the Soviet Union and its
   surrogates from the Southern African region.
5. Settlement of the South-West African problem in such
   a way that a moderate government, well-disposed towards the United States of America, should come into
   existence in the Territory.
6. Avoidance of escalating conflict in the Southern African region which would be inimical to U.S. interests.
7. Access to naval and civilian port facilities for American naval vessels.
8. Endorsing and strengthening South Africa's capacity
   to undertake naval responsibility in the South Atlantic
   and Indian Ocean and in the Southern African
   region.
9. The establishment of a stable regional environment in
   Southern Africa, well-disposed towards the U.S.A.
10. Encouraging South Africa to accommodate the na-
    tional aspirations of all its peoples in a way which will
    ensure advancement for them all and avoid conflict
    between them.

11. Recognizing that there are not short-cut solutions to the question of the exercise of political power in South Africa.

6) SOUTH AFRICAN DOCUMENT ON U.S.–SOUTH AFRICAN NUCLEAR RELATIONS

Secret   *Washington, D.C.*
                                              14 May 1981

SOUTH AFRICAN–UNITED STATES NUCLEAR RELATIONS

Introduction

1. South Africa-United States nuclear relations date back to just after the second World War when the Western Allies, and in particular the United States, were in dire need of uranium for their military programmes.

In collaboration with the Combined Development Agency (CDA), South Africa developed its uranium industry to supply uranium under contract to the CDA free of safeguards. These contracts expired in the late sixties when our production reached a level of over 3,000 tons per annum. At that time the United States also placed an embargo on foreign imports of uranium to the States.

2. An Agreement for Cooperation on the Peaceful Uses of Atomic Energy with a duration of 10 years was concluded with the US in 1957. Under this Agreement the US undertook to sanction the supply of the SAFARI research reactor to South Africa and to meet the fuel requirements for this reactor under a bilateral US-SA safeguards agreement. The 1957 Agreement for Cooperation was subsequently reviewed, amended and renewed in 1962, 1967 and again in 1974. (The 1962 amendment permitted the rental of HEU for SAFARI in addition to the purchase thereof by South Africa. The agreement was renewed in 1967 for a further 10 years after South Africa had on the insistence of the USA given assurances on its policy with regard to uranium sales. The trilateral safeguards agreement between the USA, South Africa and the IAEA was also amended to ensure the continued application of safeguards after expiry of the US-SA agreement.)

In 1974 the agreement was extended from 20 to 30 years, that is until 2007, and also to provide for the supply of separating [*sic*] working units by the United States for the life of the proposed Koeberg reactors (that is for 25 years after 1982).

In terms of this arrangement a contract for enriched uranium for the Koeberg reactors was concluded with ERDA, which was later transferred to DOE.

It must be emphasized that the 1974 agreement as well as the DOE supply contracts only provided for IAEA safeguards on such facilities and on the fuel to be transferred to South Africa by the USA.

These agreements and safeguards arrangements were and are still diligently honoured by South Africa.

3. During the latter half of 1976 it became clear to South Africa that it would become increasingly difficult to obtain fuel for its research reactor (SAFARI) from the US. Although the US never refused the required export permit for a batch of fuel, at that time on order and paid for by South Africa, unacceptable delays were experienced resulting in the cancellation of the order by South Africa when it became evident in 1977 that the delivery of the fuel would not be allowed by the previous US Administration.

4. In June of 1978 discussions took place in Pretoria on nuclear relations between the US and South Africa. During these discussions it became abundantly clear that the US would not supply the fuel in question unless South Africa acceded to NPT and subjected all its nuclear facilities and activities to international safeguards. More restrictive conditions were thus imposed unilaterally by the US after the conclusion of the contract.

5. South Africa has repeatedly stated that it will observe the principles of the NPT and also indicated that it was in principle not opposed to accession to the NPT if its basic requirements could be met.

6. Subsequent discussions to those in June 1978 revealed that even if South Africa should accede to the NPT, the US would find it difficult to provide South Africa timeously with the enriched uranium for Koeberg. South Africa was also prevented, through US intervention, from obtaining fuel from any other source unless it accepted the conditions unilaterally imposed on South Africa by the US.

The Present Position

7. Koeberg is scheduled for initial fuel loading in March 1982, and as no firm undertaking for the supply of enriched uranium could as yet

be obtained, the chances are that the scheduled start-up of Koeberg would be seriously delayed at great cost to South Africa.

The South African Position

8. (i) As has been indicated in the past, South Africa is not in principle opposed to the NPT, provided that its **basic requirements** can be met.

(ii) As in the past, South Africa will continue to conduct and administer its nuclear affairs in a manner which is in line with the spirit, principles and goals of the NPT.

(iii) South Africa's nuclear programmes are geared to the peaceful application of nuclear energy and at no time has she tested a nuclear device.

9. It must be realized that South Africa is threatened by the USSR and its associates and by certain African countries with Soviet support and encouragement. South Africa has no hope of any assistance from the UN in case of attack. On the contrary, it is continually being threatened with action under Chapter VII of the Charter of the United Nations. While this state of affairs continues South Africa cannot in the interest of its own security sign the NPT and thus set the minds of its would-be attackers at rest, allowing them to proceed freely with their plans against us.

What South Africa Requests

10. (a) That the United States Government give an undertaking that export permits will be issued for delivery of enriched uranium to France;

(b) If the US feels it cannot supply the enriched uranium through France timeously [sic] for the Koeberg reactors in present circumstances, the US makes it known to France that it would not insist on the conditions that it imposed unilaterally on South Africa after the signature of the original supply contracts if France were to supply the fuel; and

(c) DOE agrees either to cancel the present contract for the supply of enriched uranium to ESCOM at no cost, or DOE agrees to postpone execution of the contract at no cost until such time as an agreement can be reached between the United States and South African authorities which would permit the United States to resume deliveries of fuel to South Africa.

APPENDIX B

Congressional Letter to
South African Ambassador, December 4, 1984

CONGRESS OF THE UNITED STATES
HOUSE OF REPRESENTATIVES
Washington, D.C. 20515

December 4, 1984

The Honorable Bernardus G. Fourie, Ambassador
  Extraordinary and Plenipotentiary
Office of the Embassy of the Republic of South Africa
3051 Massachusetts Avenue
Washington, D.C. 20006

Dear Ambassador Fourie:

Events of recent weeks in South Africa have raised serious questions about your government's willingness to move more progressively and aggressively toward real human rights reforms. With this letter we wish to make clear that we view the violence in your country and the questions raised by it with alarm. Furthermore, we want you to know that we are prepared to pursue policy changes relative to South Africa's relationships with the United States if the situation does not improve.

We are, for the most part, politically conservative and as conservatives recognize all too well the importance and strategic value of South Africa. We understand the need for stability both within the internal affairs of your country and your external relationship with the United States. But precisely because we do feel strongly about our mutual interests, we cannot condone policies of apartheid which we believe weaken your long-term interests and certainly our ability to deal with you in a constructive manner.

The Reagan Administration has dealt with your nation on the basis of "constructive engagement." That policy merits our support as long as real steps toward complete equality for all South Africans are ongoing. If "constructive engagement" becomes in your view an excuse for maintaining the unacceptable status quo, it will quickly become an approach that can engender no meaningful support among American policy-makers.

We are looking for an immediate end to the violence in South Africa accompanied by a demonstrated sense of urgency about ending apartheid. If such actions are not forthcoming, we are prepared to recommend that the U.S. government take the following two steps:

1) Curtail new American investment in South Africa unless certain economic and civil rights guarantees for all persons are in place.

2) Organize international diplomatic and economic sanctions against South Africa.

In closing, let us reiterate our strong view that an end to apartheid is instrumental to the maintenance and growth of the relationship between South Africa and the United States. We wish to be able to endorse policies that produce stronger ties between our two nations. But the reality of apartheid and the violence used to keep it in place make it likely that our relations will deteriorate. Those obstacles to a constructive alliance must be ended.

Sincerely,

Signers of Letter
HOUSE OF REPRESENTATIVES

Representative	*State*
Vin Weber	Minnesota
Dan Coats	Indiana
Bill Goodling	Pennsylvania
John Hiler	Indiana
Richard Armey	Texas
Robert Walker	Pennsylvania
Robert Dornan	California
Benjamin Gilman	New York
George Gekas	Pennsylvania
Barbara Vucanovich	Nevada
Robert Lagomarsino	California
Connie Mack	Florida

Newt Gingrich	Georgia
Tom Bliley	Virginia
Bill Dannemeyer	California
Bob Livingston	Louisiana
Duncan Hunter	California
Jim Courter	New Jersey
Bill McCollum	Florida
Mike DeWine	Ohio
Nancy Johnson	Connecticut
Frank Wolf	Virginia
Mickey Edwards	Oklahoma
Lynn Martin	Illinois
Tom Lewis	Florida
Bobbi Fiedler	California
Steve Gunderson	Wisconsin
Chalmers Wylie	Ohio
Mark Siljander	Michigan
Ed Zschau	California
Tom Ridge	Pennsylvania
Bill Thomas	California
Bill Clinger	Pennsylvania
Rod Chandler	Washington
John Rowland	Connecticut

APPENDIX C

Address by President Ronald Reagan,
July 22, 1986

U.S. Docs: 1986

Current Policy
No. 853

ENDING APARTHEID IN SOUTH AFRICA

United States Department of State
Bureau of Public Affairs
Washington, D.C.

Following is an address by President Reagan before members of the World Affairs Council and Foreign Policy Association in the East Room of the White House, Washington, D.C., July 22, 1986.

For more than a year now, the world's attention has been focused upon South Africa—the deepening political crisis there, the widening cycle of violence. And, today, I'd like to outline American policy toward that troubled republic and toward the region of which it is a part—a region of vital importance to the West.

The root cause of South Africa's disorder is apartheid—that rigid system of racial segregation, wherein black people have been treated as third-class citizens in a nation they helped to build.

America's view of apartheid has been, and remains, clear. Apartheid is morally wrong and politically unacceptable. The United States cannot maintain cordial relations with a government whose power rests upon the denial of rights to a majority of its people based on race. If South Africa wishes to belong to the family of Western nations, an end to apartheid is a precondition. Americans, I believe, are united in this conviction. Second, apartheid must be dismantled. Time is running out for the moderates of all races in South Africa.

But if we Americans are agreed upon the goal, a free and multiracial South Africa associated with free nations and the West, there is deep disagreement about how to reach it.

First, a little history—for a quarter century now, the American Government has been separating itself from the South African Government. In 1962, President Kennedy imposed an embargo on military sales. Last September, I issued an Executive order further restricting U.S. dealings with the Pretoria government. For the past 18 months, the marketplace has been sending unmistakable signals of its own. U.S. bank lending to South Africa has been virtually halted. No significant new investment has come in. Some Western businessmen have packed up and gone home.

The Call for Sanctions

And now, we've reached a critical juncture. Many in Congress and some in Europe are clamoring for sweeping sanctions against South Africa. The Prime Minister of Great Britain has denounced punitive sanctions as "immoral" and "utterly repugnant." Well, let me tell you why we believe Mrs. Thatcher is right.

The primary victims of an economic boycott of South Africa would be the very people we seek to help. Most of the workers who would lose jobs because of sanctions would be black workers. We do not believe the way to help the people of South Africa is to cripple the economy upon which they and their families depend for survival.

Alan Paton, South Africa's great writer, for years the conscience of his country, has declared himself emphatically: "I am totally opposed to disinvestment," he says. "It is primarily for a moral reason. Those who will pay most grievously for disinvestment will be the black workers of South Africa. I take very seriously the teachings of the gospels. In particular, the parables about giving drink to the thirsty and food to the hungry. I will not help to cause any such suffering to any black person." Nor will we.

Looking at a map, southern Africa is a single economic unit tied together by rails and roads. Zaire and its southern mining region depends upon South Africa for three-fourths of its food and petroleum. More than half the electric power that drives the capital of Mozambique comes from South Africa. Over one-third of the exports from Zambia and 65% of the exports of Zimbabwe leave the continent through South African ports.

The mines of South Africa employ 13,000 workers from Swaziland, 19,000 from Botswana, 50,000 from Mozambique, and 110,000 from the tiny, landlocked country of Lesotho. Shut down these productive mines with sanctions, and you have forced black mine workers out of their jobs and forced their families back in their home countries into destitution. I don't believe the American people want to do something like that. As one African leader remarked recently, "Southern Africa is like a zebra. If the white parts are injured, the black parts die too."

Well, Western nations have poured billions in foreign aid and investment loans into southern Africa. Does it make sense to aid these countries with one hand and with the other to smash the industrial engine upon which their future depends?

Wherever blacks seek equal opportunity, higher wages, and better working conditions, their strongest allies are the American, British, French, German, and Dutch businessmen who bring to South Africa ideas of social justice formed in their own countries.

If disinvestment is mandated, these progressive Western forces will depart and South African proprietors will inherit, at fire sale prices, their farms and factories and plants and mines. And how would this end apartheid?

Our own experience teaches us that racial progress comes swiftest and easiest not during economic depression but in times of prosperity and growth. Our own history teaches us that capitalism is the natural enemy of such feudal institutions as apartheid.

Violence and Change

Nevertheless, we share the outrage Americans have come to feel. Night after night, week after week, television has brought us reports of violence by South African security forces, bringing injury and death to peaceful demonstrators and innocent bystanders. More recently, we read of violent attacks by blacks against blacks. Then, there is the calculated terror by elements of the African National Congress: the mining of roads, the bombings of public places, designed to bring about further repression—the imposition of martial law and eventually creating the conditions for racial war.

The most common method of terror is the so-called necklace. In this barbaric way of reprisal, a tire is filled with kerosene or gasoline, placed around the neck of an alleged "collaborator," and ignited.

The victim may be a black policeman, a teacher, a soldier, a civil servant. It makes no difference. The atrocity is designed to terrorize blacks into ending all racial cooperation and to polarize South Africa as prelude to a final, climactic struggle for power.

In defending their society and people, the South African Government has a right and responsibility to maintain order in the face of terrorists. But by its tactics, the government is only accelerating the descent into bloodletting. Moderates are being trapped between the intimidation of radical youths and countergangs of vigilantes.

And the government's state of emergency next went beyond the law of necessity. It, too, went outside the law by sweeping up thousands of students, civic leaders, church leaders, and labor leaders, thereby contributing to further radicalization. Such repressive measures will bring South Africa neither peace nor security.

It's a tragedy that most Americans only see or read about the dead and injured in South Africa—from terrorism, violence, and repression. For behind the terrible television pictures lies another truth: South Africa is a complex and diverse society in a state of transition. More and more South Africans have come to recognize that change is essential for survival. The realization has come hard and late; but the realization has finally come to Pretoria that apartheid belongs to the past.

In recent years, there's been a dramatic change. Black workers have been permitted to unionize, bargain collectively, and build the strongest free trade union movement in all of Africa. The infamous pass laws have been ended, as have many of the laws denying blacks the right to live, work, and own property in South Africa's cities. Citizenship, wrongly stripped away, has been restored to nearly 6 million blacks. Segregation in universities and public facilities is being set aside. Social apartheid laws prohibiting interracial sex and marriage have been struck down. It is because State President Botha has presided over these reforms that extremists have denounced him as a traitor.

We must remember, as British historian Paul Johnson reminds us, that South Africa is an African country as well as a Western country. And reviewing the history of that continent in the quarter century since independence, historian Johnson does not see South Africa as a failure: ". . . only in South Africa," he writes, "have the real incomes of blacks risen very substantially. . . . In mining, black wages have tripled in real terms in the last decade. . . . South Africa is the . . . only African country to produce a large black middle class. Almost certainly," he adds, "there are now more black women professionals in South Africa than in the whole of the rest of Africa put together."

Despite apartheid, tens of thousands of black Africans migrate into South Africa from neighboring countries to escape poverty and take advantage of the opportunities in an economy that produces nearly a third of the income in all of sub-Saharan Africa.

It's tragic that in the current crisis social and economic progress has been arrested. And, yet, in contemporary South Africa—before the state of emergency—there was a broad measure of freedom of speech, of the press, and of religion there. Indeed, it's hard to think of a single country in the Soviet bloc—or many in the United Nations—where political critics have the same freedom to be heard as did outspoken critics of the South African Government.

But, by Western standards, South Africa still falls short, terribly short, on the scales of economic and social justice.

South Africa's actions to dismantle apartheid must not end now. The state of emergency must be lifted. There must be an opening of the political process. That the black people of South Africa should have a voice in their own governance is an idea whose time has come. There can be no turning back. In the multiracial society that is South Africa, no single race can monopolize the reins of political power.

Black churches, black unions, and, indeed, genuine black nationalists have a legitimate role to play in the future of their country. But the South African Government is under no obligation to negotiate the future of the country with any organization that proclaims a goal of creating a communist state and uses terrorist tactics and violence to achieve it.

U.S. Ideals and Strategic Interests

Many Americans, understandably, ask: given the racial violence, the hatred, why not wash our hands and walk away from that tragic continent and bleeding country? Well, the answer is: we cannot.

In southern Africa, our national ideals and strategic interests come together. South Africa matters because we believe that all men are created equal and are endowed by their creator with unalienable rights. South Africa matters because of who we are. One of eight Americans can trace his ancestry to Africa.

Strategically, this is one of the most vital regions of the world. Around the Cape of Good Hope passes the oil of the Persian Gulf, which is indispensable to the industrial economies of Western Europe. Southern Africa and South Africa are repository of many of the vital minerals—vanadium, manganese, chromium, platinum—for which the West has no other secure source of supply.

The Soviet Union is not unaware of the stakes. A decade ago, using an army of Cuban mercenaries provided by Fidel Castro, Moscow installed a client regime in Angola. Today, the Soviet Union is providing that regime with the weapons to attack UNITA [National Union for the Total Independence of Angola]—a black liberation movement which seeks for Angolans the same right to be represented in their government that black South Africans seek for themselves.

Apartheid threatens our vital interests in southern Africa, because it's drawing neighboring states into the vortex of violence. Repeatedly, within the last 18 months, South African forces have struck into neighboring states. I repeat our condemnation of such behavior. Also, the Soviet-armed guerrillas of the African National Congress—operating both within South Africa and from some neighboring countries—have embarked upon new acts of terrorism inside South Africa. I also condemn that behavior.

But South Africa cannot shift the blame for these problems onto the neighboring states, especially when those neighbors take steps to stop guerrilla actions from being mounted from their own territory.

If this rising hostility in southern Africa—between Pretoria and the frontline states—explodes, the Soviet Union will be the main beneficiary. And the critical ocean corridor of South Africa and the strategic minerals of the region would be at risk. Thus, it would be a historic act of folly for the United States and the West—out of anguish and frustration and anger—to write off South Africa.

Key to the Future

Ultimately, however, the fate of South Africa will be decided there, not here. We Americans stand ready to help. But whether South Africa emerges democratic and free or takes a course leading to a downward spiral of poverty and repression will finally be their choice, not ours.

The key to the future lies with the South African Government. As I urge Western nations to maintain communication and involvement in South Africa, I urge Mr. Botha not to retreat into the *laager,* not to cut off contact with the West. Americans and South Africans have never been enemies, and we understand the apprehension and fear and concern of all your people. But an end to apartheid does not necessarily mean an end to the social, economic, and physical security of the white people in this country they love and have sacrificed so much to build.

To the black, "colored," and Asian peoples of South Africa, too long treated as second- and third-class subjects, I can only say: in your hopes for freedom, social justice, and self-determination, you have a friend and ally in the United States. Maintain your hopes for peace and reconciliation, and we will do our part to keep that road open.

We understand that behind the rage and resentment in the townships is the memory of real injustices inflicted upon generations of South Africans. Those to whom evil is done, the poet wrote, often do evil in return.

But if the people of South Africa are to have a future in a free country where the rights of all are respected, the desire for retribution will have to be set aside. Otherwise, the future will be lost in a bloody quarrel over the past.

Components for Progress Toward Peace

It would be an act of arrogance to insist that uniquely American ideas and institutions, rooted in our own history and traditions, be transplanted to South African soil. Solutions to South Africa's political crisis must come from South Africans themselves. Black and white, "colored" and Asian, they have their own traditions. But let me outline what we believe are necessary components of progress toward political peace.

- **First,** a timetable for elimination of apartheid laws should be set.
- **Second,** all political prisoners should be released.
- **Third,** Nelson Mandela should be released—to participate in the country's political process.
- **Fourth,** black political movements should be unbanned.
- **Fifth,** both the government and its opponents should begin a dialogue about constructing a political system that rests upon the consent of the governed—where the rights of majorities and minorities, and individuals are protected by law. And the dialogue should be initiated by those with power and authority—the South African Government itself.
- **Sixth,** if postapartheid South Africa is to remain the economic locomotive of southern Africa, its strong and

developed economy must not be crippled. And, therefore, I urge Congress—and the countries of Western
Europe—to resist this emotional clamor for punitive
sanctions.

If Congress imposes sanctions, it would destroy America's flexibility, discard our diplomatic leverage, and deepen the crisis. To
make a difference, Americans—who are a force for decency and
progress in the world—must remain involved. We must stay and
work, not cut and run.

It should be our policy to build in South Africa, not to bring
down. Too often in the past, we Americans—acting out of anger and
frustration and impatience—have turned our backs on flawed re-
gimes, only to see disaster follow.

Those who tell us the moral thing to do is to embargo the South
African economy and write off South Africa should tell us exactly
what they believe will rise in its place. What foreign power would fill
the vacuum if South Africa's ties with the West are broken?

The Need for Coordination

To be effective, however, our policy must be coordinated with our
key Western allies and with the front-line states in southern Africa.
These countries have the greatest concern and potential leverage on
the situation in South Africa. I intend to pursue the following steps.

- Secretary Shultz has already begun intensive consulta-
  tions with our Western allies—whose roots and presence
  in South Africa are greater than our own—on ways to
  encourage internal negotiations. We want the process to
  begin now, and we want open channels to all the principal parties. The key nations of the West must act in
  concert. And, together, we can make the difference.
- We fully support the current efforts of the British Government to revive hopes for negotiations. Foreign Secretary Howe's visits with South Africa's leader this week will
  be of particular significance.
- And second, I urge the leaders of the region to join us in
  seeking a future South Africa where countries live in
  peace and cooperation. South Africa is the nation where
  the industrial revolution first came to Africa; its economy is a mighty engine that could pull southern Africa

into a prosperous future. The other nations of southern Africa—from Kinshasa to the Cape—are rich in natural resources.

- Third, I have directed Secretary Shultz and AID [Agency for International Development] Administrator McPherson to undertake a study of America's assistance role in southern Africa to determine what needs to be done and what can be done to expand the trade, private investment, and transport prospects of southern Africa's landlocked nations. In the past 5 years, we have provided almost $1 billion in assistance to South Africa's neighbors. And this year we hope to provide an additional $45 million to black South Africans.

We're determined to remain involved, diplomatically and economically, with all the states of southern Africa that wish constructive relations with the United States.

This Administration is not only against broad economic sanctions and against apartheid; we are for a new South Africa, a new nation where all that has been built up over generations is not destroyed, a new society where participation in the social, cultural, and political life is open to all people—a new South Africa that comes home to the family of free nations where it belongs.

To achieve that, we need not a Western withdrawal but deeper involvement by the Western business community, as agents of change and progress and growth. The international business community needs not only to be supported in South Africa but energized. We'll be at work on that task. If we wish to foster the process of transformation, one of the best vehicles for change is through the involvement of black South Africans in business, job-related activities, and labor unions.

But the vision of a better life cannot be realized so long as apartheid endures and instability reigns in South Africa. If the peoples of southern Africa are to prosper, leaders and peoples of the region—of all races—will have to elevate their common interests above their ethnic divisions.

We and our allies cannot dictate to the government of a sovereign nation. Nor should we try. But we can offer to help find a solution that is fair to all the people of South Africa. We can volunteer to stand by and help bring about dialogue between leaders of the various factions and groups that make up the population of South Africa. We can counsel and advise and make it plain to all that we are there as friends of all the people of South Africa.

In that tormented land, the window remains open for peaceful change. For how long, we know not. But we in the West, privileged and prosperous and free, must not be the ones to slam it shut. Now is a time for healing. The people of South Africa, of all races, deserve a chance to build a better future. And we must not deny or destroy that chance.

Published by the United States Department of State, Bureau of Public Affairs, Office of Public Communication, Editorial Division, Washington, D.C., July 1986.

APPENDIX D
Summary of the Comprehensive Anti-Apartheid Act
of 1986 (H.R. 4868)

MAJOR SANCTIONS

Scope (Sec. 3)
All provisions of the bill apply to South Africa (including the homelands) and Namibia.

Landing Rights (Sec. 306)
Requires an immediate termination of landing rights for South African aircraft and prohibits U.S. civil aircraft from flying to South Africa.

New Investments (Sec. 310)
Prohibits any new investment in South Africa, except for investments in black-owned firms. This includes bank loans to the private sector. The term new investment does not include expenses incurred by U.S. companies to comply with the Sullivan-related fair labor standards. The prohibition does not apply to:

(1) short-term trade financing (e.g., letters of credit)
(2) most rescheduling of existing loans
(3) reinvestments of profits
(4) transfers of funds necessary to maintain operations in an economically sound manner without expanding operations.

Government Loans (Sec. 305)
Prohibits all loans to the South African Government (including parastatals), with an exception for certain loans for educational, housing or humanitarian purposes.

Parastatal Imports (Sec. 303)

Prohibits the import of any item produced, grown, manufactured, marketed, or exported by SAG parastatals (i.e., organizations owned, controlled, or subsidized by the SAG). An exception is provided for imports of articles pursuant to contracts signed before August 15, 1986, provided that no shipment of such articles may be received after April 1, 1987.

Krugerrand Imports (Sec. 301)

Prohibits the import of Krugerrands and other gold coins minted in South Africa as well as Soviet gold coins.

Imports Generally (Sec. 309; 319; 320)

Prohibits the import of South African (1) uranium ore; (2) uranium oxide;(3) coal; and (4) textiles. These import prohibitions enter into effect 90 days after enactment. The bill also prohibits the import of (5) agricultural commodities and their derivatives and any product suitable for human consumption; (6) iron; and (7) steel. The import prohibitions on the latter three products enter into force upon enactment.

Defense Imports (Sec. 302)

Prohibits the import of defense articles and data produced in South Africa.

Philippines/Sugar (Sec. 323)

In addition to the broad ban on agricultural products, the bill contains a specific prohibition on the import of South African sugar, syrups, and molasses, effective on the date of enactment. The bill also increases the Philippines' quota for such products by an amount corresponding to the South African amount.

Double Taxation (Sec. 313)

Requires the termination of the bilateral tax treaty and the related protocol in force with South Africa. The relevant provision does not terminate the provisions in the U.S. Code conferring certain double taxation credit/deductions benefits to U.S. firms/nationals regardless of tax treaties.

Government Procurement (Sec. 314)

Prohibits U.S. Government procurement from parastatals except for items necessary for diplomatic or consular purposes.

Bank Accounts (Sec. 308)

Prohibits the SAG and its parastatals from having bank accounts in the United States, with the exception of those authorized by the U.S. Government for diplomatic and consular purposes.

USG Assistance for Trade (Sec. 316)

Prohibits U.S. Government assistance for investment for trade in South Africa, including subsidies and funding for any trade missions/trade fairs.

Tourism (Sec. 315)

Prohibits the use of U.S. Government funds for the promotion of tourism in South Africa.

Computer Exports (Sec. 304)

Prohibits the export of computers and related goods and services to the police, military, and apartheid-enforcing entities.

Nuclear Exports/Trade (Sec. 307)

Prohibits most nuclear exports/trade involving South Africa (with narrow exceptions for IAEA and for humanitarian/health purposes).

Munitions Exports (Sec. 317; 318)

Prohibits the export of any item on the U.S. Munitions List (part of the International Traffic in Arms Regulations (ITAR) of the Department of State) to South Africa. Any exception is provided for items not covered by the mandatory U.N. arms embargo if the items are to be used strictly for commercial purposes and are not destined for the military, police, or security forces or military uses. This provision codifies existing Executive Branch policy. The current statutory procedures relating to the President's certification of certain ITAR exports and Congressional disapproval of individual exports are made applicable to such South Africa exports.

Oil Exports (Sec. 321)

Prohibits exports of crude oil and petroleum products to South Africa (with an exception for existing contracts).

Agricultural Exports (Sec. 212)

The bill permits South Africa to participate in Department of Agriculture export credit and promotion programs. This could include credit and loan guarantee programs and the export enhancement program recently used with respect to the USSR.

Fair Labor Standards (Sec. 205; 207; 208)

Requires U.S. nationals employing at least 25 individuals in South Africa to apply certain fair labor standards based on the Sullivan principles. The penalty for failure to implement the principles is a loss of U.S. Government export marketing support. (These provisions are comparable to those in the September 9, 1985, Executive Order.) The U.S. Embassy and Consulates in South Africa are also required to implement the principles, except that the bill makes it clear that the applicable provision does not confer a right to engage in strikes against the U.S. Government.

Unfair Trade Practices (Sec. 402)

The bill authorizes the President to limit the import into the United States of any products of any foreign country to the extent that the country concerned benefits from or otherwise takes commercial advantage of the sanctions contained in the the bill.

Private Cause of Action (Sec. 403)

Under certain very limited circumstances, the bill permits U.S. nationals to bring civil suits for damages in U.S. courts against foreign corporations or individuals which take advantage of the U.S. sanctions contained in the bill.

Preemption (Sec. 4; 606)

The Senate bill establishes a comprehensive and complete U.S. framework for dealing with South Africa. The Senate legislative history makes it clear that state and local legislative sanctions against South Africa (e.g., procurement bans against U.S. firms doing business in South Africa) are preempted by the bill for purposes of U.S. law. The bill contains a transitional amendment which provides in effect that states will not be punished for acts taken as a result of such laws currently in force for a period of 90 days.

Waivers (Sec. 311; 502)

The bill contains several provisions regarding Presidential waivers or modifications of the bill. One provision authorizes waivers if certain events occur in South Africa, provided that the Congress does not enact a joint resolution of disapproval (which can be vetoed).

International Negotiations (Sec. 401)

The bill requires negotiations with other countries within 180 days on international arrangements to end apartheid. It provides that the secretary of state should convene an international conference to reach agreements and impose multilateral sanctions (as well as certain reporting requirements). Presidential modifications of the bill as a result of such agreements will require congressional approval by joint resolution.

UN Mandatory Sanctions (Sec. 401)

The bill expresses the sense of the Congress that the President should seek mandatory Chapter VII Security Council sanctions against South Africa of the kind contained in the bill.

Waivers/Communist Countries (Sec. 502)

The bill provides that the President may lift any prohibition in the bill if it would increase U.S. dependence upon any member country or observer country of the Council for Mutual Economic Assistance (i.e., the economic entity related to the Warsaw Pact) for the import of (1) coal or (2) any strategic material or (3) any critical material. Criteria are established for this purpose. Although many reports must be made to Congress (including monthly reports), there is no procedure for Congressional disapproval or approval of such Presidential determinations.

Military Cooperation (Sec. 322)

The bill prohibits any agency or entity of the U.S. Government from engaging in any form of cooperation with the armed forces of South Africa, except activities reasonably designed to facilitate the collection of necessary intelligence.

Future Sanctions (Sec. 501)

Requires the President to make a report to Congress 12 months after enactment on progress in South Africa. If he determines that the conditions specified have not been met, the bill requires that the President must recommend which additional measures should be adopted (from a list of potential sanctions). The sanctions are not automatic, and a law would have to be enacted to promulgate any sanctions recommended by the President pursuant to these procedures. The future measures could include prohibitions on military assistance to countries violating the U.N. arms embargo; the import of diamonds and strategic minerals; and the holding of any U.S. bank accounts for South Africa nationals.

POSITIVE MEASURES

Scholarships/Assistance (Sec. 201; 511)

Authorizes assistance for scholarships to the victims of apartheid and assistance generally for disadvantaged South Africans. For example, one provision provides that up to 40 million dollars in economic support funds may be used in FY87 and each year thereafter for assistance in South Africa. Another earmarks 4 million dollars of the education funds available to the U.S. Agency for International Development for each of the fiscal years 1987 through 1989 for scholarship programs at the university/college level. A separate provision authorizes 1 million dollars in each of the fiscal years 1987 through 1989 for scholarships for secondary school students. A separate training program for teachers is also authorized.

Legal Assistance/Human Rights Fund (Sec. 202)

Earmarks specific amounts of the Human Rights Fund for South Africa for specified purposes (500,000 dollars per fiscal year for legal assistance to political prisoners and detainees, and 175,000 dollars for families of the victims of those necklaced).

Export-Import Bank (Sec. 204)

Requires EXIM to take active steps to encourage the use of its facilities to assist black South Africa business enterprises and relaxes certain current statutory restrictions on EXIM activities in South Africa.

Housing (Sec. 206)

Authorizes 10 million dollars for the purchase of housing for black South Africa nationals employed by the U.S. Government in South Africa. The housing is to be located in areas open to all population groups.

USG Procurement (Sec. 203)

Provides that the U.S. Embassy and Consulates in South Africa shall make affirmative efforts to purchase goods and services from the victims of apartheid notwithstanding normal competition in contracting laws.

African Famine Reserve (Sec. 210)

The President is authorized to use the Emergency Reserve for African Famine Relief established as part of the P.L. 480 program notwithstanding certain existing legal requirements.

REPORTING REQUIREMENTS

The bill contains numerous reporting requirements, including reports relating to the following:

Role/activities of the Communist Party in South Africa (§509)

Countries violating the Mandatory UN Arms Embargo (§508)

Health conditions in the homelands (§503)

Effect of sanctions on Front Line States (§505)

Bank deposits of South Africans in the U.S. (§507)

South African Imports/Strategic minerals (§504)

CEMA (Warsaw pact-related) imports (§502)

African National Congress compliance with the Foreign Agents Registration Act (§512)

Strategy for assisting disadvantaged South Africans over the next 5 years (§511)

POLICY STATEMENTS

The Senate bill contains numerous policy statements, including praise for U.S. firms that have remained to work in South Africa; the need for negotiations in South Africa and to have all foreign forces removed from the region; and the need for international cooperation and coordination on measures related to South Africa. Other examples including the following.

African National Congress (Sec. 102; 311)

The bill provides that U.S. policy toward the African National Congress (ANC) shall be designed to bring about a suspension of violence that will lead to the start of negotiations designed to bring about a non-racial and genuine democracy in South Africa. The United States is to encourage the ANC to (1) suspend terrorist activities; (2) make known its commitment to a free and democratic post-apartheid South Africa; (3) agree to enter into negotiations; and (4) reexamine its ties to the South African Communist party. It also provides that U.S. policy towards South Africa will be adjusted based on certain actions of both the SAG and the ANC. It provides that it shall be the policy of the U.S. to support negotiations without the ANC if the SAG agrees to enter into negotiations without conditions and abandons unprovoked violence and commits itself to a free and democratic post-apartheid South Africa, and if the ANC (1) refuses to participate in negotiations or (2) if the ANC refuses to abandon unprovoked violence during such negotiations and refuses to commit itself to a free and democratic post-apartheid South Africa.

Mandela Meeting (Sec. 109)

The bill expresses the sense of the Congress that the U.S. Ambassador to South Africa should meet with Nelson Mandela.

ENFORCEMENT (Sec. 603; 601)

Severe criminal and civil penalties are provided for violations of the bill and broad regulatory powers are conferred on the President.

TERMINATION (Sec. 311)

The bill provides that the sanctions contained in the bill shall terminate automatically if the SAG meets five conditions specified in the bill. These conditions related to (1) the release of Nelson Mandela and all political prisoners; (2) the repeal of the State of Emergency and all detainees; (3) the unbanning of political parties; (4) the repeal of the Group Areas and Population Registration Acts; and (5) agreeing to enter into good faith negotiations with truly representative members of the black majority without preconditions.

Source: Working files of the Secretary of State's Advisory Committee on Africa.

APPENDIX E

Agreements for Peace in Southwestern Africa,
December 22, 1988

Selected Documents
No. 32

December 1988

United States Department of State
Bureau of Public Affairs
Washington, D.C.

TRIPARTITE AGREEMENT, DECEMBER 22, 1988

*AGREEMENT AMONG THE PEOPLE'S REPUBLIC OF ANGOLA, THE
REPUBLIC OF CUBA, AND THE REPUBLIC OF SOUTH AFRICA*

The Governments of the People's Republic of Angola, the Republic
of Cuba, and the Republic of South Africa, hereinafter designated as
"the Parties,"

Taking into account the "Principles for a Peaceful Settlement in
Southwestern Africa," approved by the Parties on 20 July 1988, and
the subsequent negotiations with respect to the implementation of
these Principles, each of which is indispensable to a comprehensive
settlement,

Considering the acceptance by the Parties of the implementation of United Nations Security Council Resolution 435 (1978),
adopted on 29 September 1978, hereinafter designated as "UNSCR
435/78,"

Considering the conclusion of the bilateral agreement between
the People's Republic of Angola and the Republic of Cuba providing
for the redeployment toward the North and the staged and total
withdrawal of Cuban troops from the territory of the People's Republic of Angola,

Recognizing the role of the United Nations Security Council in implementing UNSCR 435/78 and in supporting the implementation of the present agreement,

Affirming the sovereignty, sovereign equality, and independence of all states of southwestern Africa,

Affirming the principle of non-interference in the internal affairs of states,

Affirming the principle of abstention from the threat or use of force against the territorial integrity or political independence of states,

Reaffirming the right of the peoples of the southwestern region of Africa to self-determination, independence, and equality of rights, and of the states of southwestern Africa to peace, development, and social progress,

Urging African and international cooperation for the settlement of the problems of the development of the southwestern region of Africa,

Expressing their appreciation for the mediating role of the Government of the United States of America,

Desiring to contribute to the establishment of peace and security in southwestern Africa,

Agree to the provisions set forth below:

(1) The Parties shall immediately request the Secretary-General of the United Nations to seek authority from the Security Council to commence implementation of UNSCR 435/78 on 1 April 1989.

(2) All military forces of the Republic of South Africa shall depart Namibia in accordance with UNSCR 435/78.

(3) Consistent with the provisions of UNSCR 435/78, the Republic of South Africa and People's Republic of Angola shall cooperate with the Secretary-General to ensure the independence of Namibia through free and fair elections and shall abstain from any action that could prevent the execution of UNSCR 435/78. The Parties shall respect the territorial integrity and inviolability of borders of Namibia and shall ensure that their territories are not used by any state, organization, or person in connection with acts of war, aggression, or violence against the territorial integrity or inviolability of borders of Namibia or any other action which could prevent the execution of UNSCR 435/78.

(4) The People's Republic of Angola and the Republic of Cuba shall implement the bilateral agreement, signed on the date of signature of this agreement, providing for the redeployment toward the North and the staged and total withdrawal of Cuban troops from the territory of the People's Republic of Angola, and the arrange-

ments made with the Security Council of the United Nations for the on-site verification of that withdrawal.

(5) Consistent with their obligations under the Charter of the United Nations, the Parties shall refrain from the threat or use of force, and shall ensure that their respective territories are not used by any state, organization, or person in connection with any acts of war, aggression, or violence, against the territorial integrity, inviolability of borders, or independence of any state of southwestern Africa.

(6) The Parties shall respect the principle of non-interference in the internal affairs of the states of southwestern Africa.

(7) The Parties shall comply in good faith with all obligations undertaken in this agreement and shall resolve through negotiation and in a spirit of cooperation any disputes with respect to the interpretation or implementation thereof.

(8) This agreement shall enter into force upon signature.

Signed at New York in triplicate in the Portuguese, Spanish and English languages, each language being equally authentic, this 22nd day of December 1988.

FOR THE PEOPLE'S REPUBLIC OF ANGOLA
Afonso Van Dunem
FOR THE REPUBLIC OF CUBA
Isidoro Octavio Malmierca
FOR THE REPUBLIC OF SOUTH AFRICA
Roelof F. Botha

BILATERAL AGREEMENT, DECEMBER 22, 1988

Following is the unofficial U.S. translation of the original Portuguese and Spanish texts of the agreement, with annex.

AGREEMENT BETWEEN THE GOVERNMENTS OF THE PEOPLE'S REPUBLIC OF ANGOLA AND THE REPUBLIC OF CUBA FOR THE TERMINATION OF THE INTERNATIONALIST MISSION OF THE CUBAN MILITARY CONTINGENT

The Government of the People's Republic of Angola and the Republic of Cuba, hereinafter designated as the Parties,

Considering,

That the implementation of Resolution 435 of the Security Council of the United Nations for the independence of Namibia shall commence on the 1st of April,

That the question of the independence of Namibia and the safeguarding of the sovereignty, independence and territorial integrity of the People's Republic of Angola are closely interrelated with each other and with peace and security in the region of southwestern Africa,

That on the date of signature of this agreement a tripartite agreement among the Governments of the People's Republic of Angola, the Republic of Cuba and the Republic of South Africa shall be signed, containing the essential elements for the achievement of peace in the region of southwestern Africa,

That acceptance of and strict compliance with the foregoing will bring to an end the reasons which compelled the Government of the People's Rebublic of Angola to request, in the legitimate exercise of its rights under Article 51 of the United Nations Charter, the deployment to Angolan territory of a Cuban internationalist military contingent to guarantee, in cooperation with the FAPLA [the Angolan Government army], its territorial integrity and sovereignty in view of the invasion and occupation of part of its territory,

Noting,

The agreements signed by the Governments of the People's Republic of Angola and the Republic of Cuba on 4 February 1982 and 19 March 1984, the platform of the Government of the People's Repulic of Angola approved in November 1984, and the Protocol of Brazzaville signed by the Governments of the People's Republic of Angola, the Republic of Cuba and the Republic of South Africa on December 13, 1988,

Taking into account,

That conditions now exist which make possible the repatriation of the Cuban military contingent currently in Angolan territory and the successful accomplishment of their internationalist mission,

The parties agree as follows:

Article 1

To commence the redeployment by stages to the 15th and 13th parallels and the total withdrawal to Cuba of the 50,000 men who constitute the Cuban troops contingent stationed in the People's Republic of Angola, in accordance with the pace and timeframe established in the attached calendar, which is an integral part of this agreement. The total withdrawal shall be completed by the 1st of July, 1991.

Article 2

The Governments of the People's Republic of Angola and the Republic of Cuba reserve the right to modify or alter their obligations deriving from Article 1 of this Agreement in the event that flagrant violations of the Tripartite Agreement are verified.

Article 3

The Parties, through the Secretary General of the United Nations Organization, hereby request that the Security Council verify the redeployment and phased and total withdrawal of Cuban troops from the territory of the People's Repulic of Angola, and to this end shall agree on a matching protocol.

Article 4

This agreement shall enter into force upon signature of the tripartite agreement among the People's Republic of Angola, the Republic of Cuba, and the Republic of South Africa.

Signed on 22 December 1988, at the Headquarters of the United Nations Organization, in two copies, in the Portuguese and Spanish languages, each being equally authentic.

FOR THE PEOPLE'S REPUBLIC OF ANGOLA
Afonso Van Dunem
FOR THE REPUBLIC OF CUBA
Isidoro Octavio Malmierca

Annex on Troop Withdrawal Schedule

Calendar

In compliance with Article 1 of the agreement between the Government of the Republic of Cuba and the Government of the People's

Republic of Angola for the termination of the mission of the Cuban internationalist military contingent stationed in Angolan territory, the parties establish the following calendar for the withdrawal:

Time Frames

Prior to the first of April, 1989
(date of the beginning of
implementation of Resolution 435)   3,000 men

Total duration of the calendar
Starting from the 1st of April, 1989   27 months

Redeployment to the north:
to the 15th parallel   by 1 August 1989
to the 13th parallel   by 31 Oct. 1989

Total men to be withdrawn:
by 1 November 1989   25,000 men (50%)
by 1 April 1990   33,000 (66%)
by 1 October 1990   38,000 (76%);
 12,000 men
 remaining
by July 1991   50,000 (100%)

Taking as its base a Cuban force of 50,000 men.

PROVISIONS OF UN RESOLUTION 435

Following an agreement on a date to implement UN Resolution 435 and establishment of a formal cease-fire, a UN representative and a UN planning group would administer Namibia during the transition to independence in conjunction with the South African-appointed Administrator General. A UN Transitional Assistance Group (UNTAG) would supervise the cease-fire and monitor South African and South-West Africa People's Organization (SWAPO) forces.

Within three months of a cease-fire, South African forces would be reduced to 1,500 men, confined to one or two bases in northern Namibia. SWAPO forces would be restricted to specified locations in Angola under UN supervision. All political prisoners held by both sides would be released.

Seven months after the implementation date, elections would be held under UN auspices for a new constituent assembly. The remaining South African troops would depart within a few months, once elections were certified by the UN and independence granted. Unarmed SWAPO members and Namibian refugees would be permitted to return to participate in the election process.

INDEX

Author

Pauline H. Baker is a senior associate at the Carnegie Endowment for International Peace, where she writes and lectures on U.S. policy toward Africa. She received her B.A. from Douglass College, Rutgers University, and her M.A. and Ph.D. with distinction from the University of California at Los Angeles.

Dr. Baker lived in Africa for eleven years and has traveled extensively throughout the continent, including South Africa. She taught comparative government and international relations at the University of Lagos in Nigeria, 1965–1972; conducted research in southern Africa as a Rockefeller Foundation fellow, 1975–76; was a professional staff member of the U.S. Senate Foreign Relations Committee, with principal responsibility for African Affairs, 1977–81; and was a research scientist at the Battelle Memorial Institute, 1981–84. She is a member of the Council on Foreign Relations and served on the board of directors of the African Studies Association. Dr. Baker is also a professorial lecturer at The Johns Hopkins School of Advanced International Studies in Washington, D.C. She has published widely on a number of African issues.

Editor

John de St. Jorre, a journalist and author, has been visiting and writing about South Africa since the mid-1960s. His book *South Africa: A House Divided* was published by the Carnegie Endowment in New York in 1977, and he was a senior writer for the study commission that produced *South Africa: Time Running Out* in 1981.

Born in London and educated at Oxford University, he joined the British Foreign Service and spent three years in different posts in Africa. After resigning, he became the *London Observer*'s Africa correspondent, based first in Zambia and later in Kenya. He covered the Nigeria-Biafra conflict, and his book on that subject, *The Brothers' War: Biafra and Nigeria,* was published in Britain and the United States. He was subsequently the *Observer*'s Paris, Middle East, and New York correspondent, and now lives in New York City. His other books include *The Patriot Game* (a novel), *The Insider's Guide to Spain, The Guards,* and *The Marines.*